SACRED PLACES
SITES OF SPIRITUALITY & FAITH

THIS IS A CARLTON BOOK

Text and design copyright © 2007, 2012
Carlton Books Limited

This edition published in 2012
by Carlton Books Limited
20 Mortimer Street
London W1T 3JW

10 9 8 7 6 5 4 3 2 1

A CIP catalogue record for this book is available
from the British Library.

ISBN: 978-1-78097-062-2

Printed and bound in Dubai

Senior Executive Editor: Lisa Dyer
Art Editor: Anna Pow
Designer: Liz Wiffen
Copy Editor: Clare Hubbard
Picture Researcher: Jenny Meredith
Production: Ed Carter and Janette Burgin
Cover by Lucy Coley

CARLTON
BOOKS

SACRED PLACES
SITES OF SPIRITUALITY & FAITH

REBECCA HIND

CONTENTS

Introduction

Sacred places span the globe, touch and pierce its surface and vary from the intimate, private spaces known to few, to the soaring mountains and cathedrals that draw thousands. While each and every one can be located on a map and described in terms of topography, history, flora and fauna, that extra quality that takes us beyond those points of reference and onto holy ground is harder to grasp. Sacredness cannot be distilled into an easy definition; it has many facets, from the cosmic all-embracing events that transcend time and space to the minute seen and unseen renewal of life on a daily basis, which goes on in every aspect of creation. And while theologians debate the nature of the sacred within and across the faiths, many individuals have their own way of finding what connects them to the divine, through prayer, meditation, rites of passage, singing, unloading troubles and sharing joys or being with nature. The sites where we express those activities, alone or collectively, can take on a sacred aspect. It may be a place known only to us that harbours memories of a time or a person, a space that lifts the spirit and soothes troubles or a historic devotional spot that holds the prayers of generations of worshippers. A majestic landscape, the power of a mountain, the vibration of a waterfall all have their own light, colour, wildlife, scent and sound; they also have the ability to push the mundane from our thoughts and lift us to a heightened sense of awareness. Does this mean then, that some places are inherently sacred and have the ability to infuse our souls?

Perhaps there is a symbiotic relationship whereby spirituality can be generated or absorbed, according to need. The spiritual traveller will know that a sacred journey can take many forms, physical or metaphysical. Of the places we visit in this book many are ancient but all have a part to play in the spiritual life of the twenty-first century. For to ignore the past is to deprive the future and in learning of ancient traditions we come to understand their evolution into current practice. Therefore, engaging with these sites demands a leap of imagination if we are to get anywhere near to understanding other cultures' viewpoints. Only then can we learn to empathize with the needs of the world and the life that dwells here.

Throughout the world, sacred places may be connected with the mainstream faiths and here we see the great houses of worship. These are the mosques, cathedrals and temples that have been designed to concentrate the mind on God and allow the priests to educate and minister to the congregation's needs. Elsewhere, localized tribal or indigenous groups may worship in the open, finding the gods within nature. In some instances, the faith groups that originally used a site may have dwindled and the place may been adopted by another faith, by archaeologists or tourists, but that is not to devalue what has gone before. Through these pages we visit prehistoric sites where we know little or nothing of the words first spoken there, but whose people painted on cave walls with a visual language so strong and timeless that we cannot help being arrested by awe and wonder. At early burial sites we find the dead treated with reverence and care, and sent to the next life with provision for the journey. We touch waters that heal, quench and cleanse, springing from the earth as from the mouths of bountiful gods and pulling the heavenly bodies down to our level in overnight reflections. Mountain tops allow the faithful to reach as close to heaven as is physically possible in this world, where clean air and wonderful views elevate our spirits through the simple joy of looking. Similarly, pilgrim routes allow us to learn and grow in company, feel the satisfaction of arrival and the prospect of refreshment.

Our enjoyment of the beauty and value of sacred sites is enhanced if we enter with open and receptive minds, ensuring that our actions are respectful and appropriate. However, no spiritual traveller can be unaware of the need to set out with care for the environment. Condensed within this book is something of the essence of the sites it visits, so as you turn the pages, delight at the wonders and variety of creation by God, and through God, knowing that some places may be unreachable except through inner journeys.

left Sri Pada in Sri Lanka has multifaith meaning and is perhaps the only mountain where many faiths worship alongside each other. Thought to be home to guardian spirits, a mysterious giant footprint is said to mark, variously, the site of Shiva's creation dance, Buddha's presence, Adam's step when he first trod upon the earth, or Saint Thomas's arrival with Christianity.

the americas

The peoples of the continent we call America arrived from northern Asia by land bridge which joined Asia with the New World. Anthropology, DNA markers and linguistic study support the theory, although some Native Americans believe that their ancestors have lived on this continent since the beginning of time. As the population spread across the land, separate tribes and nations formed, each with its own culture and beliefs. We begin this chapter in the south and make our way up towards the Bering Strait, which thousands of years ago, may have been that prehistoric gateway.

The Temple of Kukulkan at Chichen Itzá is dedicated to the feathered serpent god and acts as a huge calendar, marking time in powerful fashion and encapsulating much of what is hallowed by the cultures we visit in this chapter. It also demonstrates the sophisticated knowledge of astronomers, mathematicians and artists as they worked together to reinforce sacred culture.

From the sacred mountain of Machu Picchu

in Peru we head north to Mexico, where we linger and consider four sites to gain an insight into a culture that continues to be expressed through ancient languages, a meld of religions and of unique world view. Then we look at the mysterious Serpent Mound, Ohio, the vast Grand Canyon, Wrangell–Saint Elias National Park and Preserve and on to the Niagara Falls.

Water is an element running through the consciousness of faith groups throughout the world, and is central to the sacred sites we visit in America. In Machu Picchu a holy spring provided fresh water to each dwelling. In dry Yucatán, Chac the rain god was crucial in bringing much-needed rainstorms to Uxmal, and at Chichen Itzá sinkholes were held sacred both for the water they brought and the gods they housed. Palenque enjoys rainforest climate and took its early name from Lama Ha, meaning 'wide water' and at Teotihuacán, Tlaloc was revered as god of rain, floods and drought.

It is true to say that Mexico is rich in many natural resources, water being one of them. Yet in some areas, Chiapas for instance, access to clean water is now limited due to various forms of pollution and industrialization. It is a cruel irony that one of the world's largest drinks manufacturers drains local water and controls access to it, while making a bottled drink that consumes huge volumes to yield relatively little product. Many of the local population are forced to choose between buying bottled water at inflated prices, resorting to the cheaper carbonated drink or chancing their luck with the little water left in the polluted natural sources. Local people are now actively responding to this gross iniquity.

It is humbling to think of the huge aquatic forces of the Colorado River, which have formed the Grand Canyon over such a long period of time, and how it now snakes its way through the landscape in a variety of moods, from the majestic to the angry flash flood. Water in its many forms plays a major part of the topography at Wrangell–Saint Elias National Park and Preserve, and the ice fields are watched with trepidation, as indicators of global warming. Here, water is hallowed for its harvest as much as for its quenching and cleansing powers. After death, water is driven from the body by heat as an essential process for entry to the Tlingit spirit world. Waterfalls are held as being sacred within many faith traditions, and the Niagara Falls are no exception to that, with their vapours lifting the souls of the dead towards the next life. Shared between the twin cities of Niagara Falls, Ontario, and Niagara Falls, New York, the Falls' energy is harvested as

hydroelectric power and an industrial landscape has grown around the area, provoking a challenge between progress and environmental preservation.

While much water comes from beneath the earth's surface, the sky is an indicator of sudden change in hydration, and early cultures had an astonishing knowledge of more than just rain clouds. They tracked the heavenly bodies such as sun, moon and Venus, and their movements became woven into every aspect of life. Machu Picchu is sited within the clouds and alignments mark the solar phases with precision. Here, at the time of equinox the sun hangs directly above the Intiwatana stone and therefore casts no shadow, giving the strange illusion of a supernatural relationship between stone and the apparently static sun. At Uxmal, legend says that the Pyramid of the Magician was built by the sky god Itzamna, while at Palenque the sky gods are depicted in stone and honoured at the Temple of the Sun. The Temple of Kukulkan at Chichen Itzá is not only a huge calendar designed to mark time, it also allows the sun to perform spectacular shadow play at certain times of year. And time is noted in similar fashion with calendrical markers at Teotihuacán, where we also find an exquisite wall painting in which voice patterns scroll into the air from figures dancing around a flying insect. The Serpent Mound at Ohio poses questions of alignment but its very size may

indicate that it was made to be seen from above, by sky gods overlooking the site. However the Hualapi tribe at the western rim of the Grand Canyon now offers tourists the chance to step out more than 21 metres (68 feet) into the sky at a height of over 12,000 metres (40,000 feet), on the glass-bottomed, horseshoe-shaped Skywalk. This gives a twenty-first century way of appreciating the grandeur of the phenomenal landscape as seen from the perspective of soaring eagles. It is also the tribe's way of generating sufficient income to sustain their existence.

Art and spirituality infuse the Tlingit people's culture and the Theft of Daylight story tells of how the sun first came to be in the sky, while at the Niagara Falls Lelawala continues to live in the mists, which rise into the air above the Horseshoe Falls. And so while the different sites we visit speak of individual faiths and concepts of the forces that shaped their belief systems, there is also much that is universal in the search for the divine and recognition of the sacred.

left to right Palenque, Mexico; Grand Canyon National Park, Arizona, USA, Wrangell–Saint Elias National Park & Preserve, Alaska; Niagara Falls, Ontario, Canada, and New York, USA.

Machu Picchu Cuzco, Peru

Throughout the world temples are formed to echo the shapes of mountains and point towards heaven. The builders of Machu Picchu went further and placed a whole worshipful city as close to the sky as they possibly could. Temples and terraces, ceremonial chambers and dwellings, hug the Andean mountain and follow its form. Here, 2,430 metres (7,972 feet) above sea level, is a setting so exquisite that the poet Pablo Neruda wrote 'Machu Picchu is a trip to the serenity of the soul, to the eternal fusion with the cosmos…'.

Ancient tradition points to society being established here by Manco Khapaq and his wife Mama Oqllu, along with tutelary spirits and sky gods. Between them they instilled rules for agriculture and craftsmanship, among many other things. Then came Inca emperor Pachakuteq, who built the citadel in the fifteenth century and who is honoured by a mausoleum in the sanctuary.

Rising from a sacred valley lush with natural beauty stands a citadel whose walls were polished and gilded by Inca artisans and whose noblest people were adorned with gold, feathers and orchids. Dedicated zones serve specific functions – a sacred one hallows the sun god Inti and another exalts priests, royalty and the Amautas, or wise elders. Among the workers' many tasks was maintenance of an irrigation system that fed sacred water from a *puquio*, or holy spring, to each dwelling in order of sanctity.

Previously known only to locals, an American explorer, Hiram Bingham, discovered the site in 1911. He noted that its very inaccessibility had saved it from the conquistadors and immediately recognized the site's spiritual purpose of venerating the dead and welcoming the sun.

Mysteriously, it was discovered that the population of the citadel was largely female. Many of their remains show signs of deliberate deformation of the skull – perhaps done in the pursuit of yet more beauty or out of a desire for fusion with the cosmos.

left This aerial photograph gives a stunning view of the vertiginous site on which Machu Picchu stands, high above the Urubamba River. The landscape here is a tropical rainforest and the citadel was built on such steep-sided mountains that terraces had to be constructed to hold it.

above Over 100 flights of stone steps climb up and down the site and many were hewn from a single granite block. It is a wonder and a mystery how such great weights were manoeuvred up the mountain without the use of the wheel and regrettable that so much practical knowledge has been lost. But in this place earthly skills combined with natural beauty, forging a harmony between man and nature. There is a momentous energy here.

above Under the Temple of the Sun, the Royal Tomb housed over 100 mummified bodies, most of them female. Here and throughout the site, an extraordinary construction technique called ashlar was used. Blocks of stone were cut in such a way that they locked together without the need for mortar. In this instance they construct a tactile sculpture of curves and contours.

above From the Sacred Plaza stairs lead to a solar observatory called the Hill of the Intiwatana – a stepped pyramid peaked by a rock cut to many angles. The Intiwatana is thought to be a solar clock. However, despite the Incas' many sophisticated skills, they used no form of writing and therefore we have no written clues as to how such instruments may have been used.

Pyramid of the Magician
Uxmal, Yucatán, Mexico

The buildings at Uxmal, the ancient Mayan city, date to between 700 and 1000 AD and their layout visualizes Mayan understanding of astronomy, time and cosmology. Still steeped in mystery, the various names of its dominant structure introduce its purpose: the Pyramid of the Magician, El Divino and Pyramid of the Soothsayer conjure visions of spiritual and supernatural forces at work in the material world. According to legend the pyramid was built overnight by Itzamna, god of the sky, darkness and light.

Elsewhere at this formerly bustling city of 25,000 people, is a building the Spaniards misnamed 'The Nunnery'. It takes the form of a quadrangle, and its name from a resemblance to European nunneries, the walls being elaborately adorned

left and below It has been said of Mayan artists that they left no space unfilled and they clearly relished the chance to affirm their culture. Mayan writing is hieroglyphic, often heavily stylized and geometric. It is also aesthetically exquisite, with some marks representing objects, sounds or concepts. The Governor's Palace, below, shows a long facade of intricate stonework, while the crosses at the bottom of the Pyramid of the Magician, left, refer to the ecliptic – the path of the sun across the sky – a significant symbol for a culture devoted to astronomy.

with astonishingly detailed decoration. These too employ cosmographic language, relating to the heavens, the gods and the structure of creation. For example, the quincunx pattern – a pattern consisting of five objects, four at the corners of a square or rectangle and the fifth in the centre, like the five on a dice – relates to the four cardinal points centred by a fifth, representing a portal to another realm and the source of creation. This pattern occurs repeatedly on the walls of the Nunnery and would have been picked out in symbolic coloured pigments, extending the visual language. This palace was probably a training place for healers, astrologers, shamans and priests.

Religious belief infused every aspect of life, binding the mundane with the celestial. In Mayan culture, grasping the past and its cyclical recurrence enables anticipation of the future. The shaman was, and still is, of prime importance in interpreting signs and acting as an intermediary between the spirit and human worlds. Visitors today may come for a light and sound show or for a festival, but many prefer to quietly soak up the atmosphere and reflect upon the art and culture in the knowledge that the Mayan tradition is still vital and playing its role in the balance of world religions.

above In shedding their skins, serpents represent rebirth. They also facilitated movement of the ancestors and were vehicles for the celestial bodies to travel through the heavens. Notice here that the rattlesnake lends its skin pattern to the surrounding stones. This repetitive geometry may have been used in scrying – shamanic divination.

above Pyramids were built to emulate the profile of sacred mountains and reach heavenward, offering astronomers great vantage points. Archaeoastronomers have calculated that in the year 760 AD, Halley's Comet would have swept close to Venus and the crescent moon. A total solar eclipse, an annular eclipse and two partial lunar eclipses would have been seen from the western steps of the Pyramid of the Magician.

above Masks of Chaac on the walls in the Nunnery Quadrangle, seen here in profile. God of rain and thunder, Chaac is also associated with agriculture and there is a reference to this encoded within the quincunx pattern (see page 17). In some regions of Mexico farmers still 'centre' their fields by marking five points, continuing a concept relating to the origins of creation.

Palenque Chiapas, Mexico

Amid the rainforests of Chiapas, crossed by the rivers and streams that led to the early name Lama Ha, or Wide Water, sits the ancient city now known as Palenque. The site was occupied for about 2,000 years, though inscriptions date the city to the late fourth century, with civilization peaking between 500 and 700 AD, during the Mayan Classical period. Artistic zeal and scientific enquiry are woven into Palenque's walls. Carvings, reliefs and colourful stucco panels all executed with creative flair and exquisite craftsmanship ennoble a city exalting the gods of rain and maize, and of the sun, moon and planet Venus. These in turn tell of a society exploring cosmology and relating cosmic pattern to cycles of growth, harvest and season. The Maya believed the god Hunab-Ku created mankind, whose first food was provided by the ceiba tree and one of these stood at each of the four corners of the earth while four gods, the *cargadores*, supported the sky. Temporal turning points were marked by ritual ceremonies involving the whole population and abundant sensory kindling. The smell of burning copal, the sounds of prayer and music, the effects of fasting and the throng of crowds are all familiar to pilgrims and worshippers today. But ancient gods demanded terrible human sacrifice in forms our culture could not condone.

Pakal the Great was the ruler whose vision and governance elevated the city to epic grandeur. His tomb, hidden for centuries and holding secrets of dynasty and deities, lies in the Temple of the Inscriptions. Named for its hieroglyphs, it is a microcosm of underworld, earth and sky.

Palenque's story continues to unfold as archaeologists brush away the layers of time and decipher what they find, while visitors relish the connection sparked by art, architecture and contemplation of the cosmos.

right Beside the forested Sierra de Don Juan is the Temple of Inscriptions and, to the left, the well-preserved Temple of the Sun, named after the Sun Jaguar of the underworld. Inside the Temple of Inscriptions another pyramid houses a stairway leading back down to ground level where, above the great ruler's tomb, a carving shows Pakal the Great tumbling down into the underworld.

above left Within the palace are four such courtyards. Vapours swirl around the forest showing the climate, hence the need for the shelters that look onto the courtyard. Stone tablets around the outside are inscribed and carved to tell of rulers, gods, ritual and the subordination of prisoners, while the interiors are lush with stucco decoration.

above The Palace is made up of 13 chambers, a tower and underground galleries. Its status is confirmed by its elevation, the content of its paintings and the presence of a throne for ritual and ceremony. However, the unique tower remains a mystery. It may have been a watchtower or a place for astronomical observation and celestial communion.

left This detail of a stone panel in the central courtyard of the palace is typical of Mayan relief work, which speaks its own arcane language. The hand on the opposite shoulder is an expression of respect or submission. Other stones show figures who still play a role in society even after death, their afterlife symbolized by their garments.

Chichen Itzá Yucatán, Mexico

Low-lying, flat and porous, the ground in Yucatán drinks water from the surface, leaving no rivers to quench the land. Thus the sinkholes, known as cenotes, that offer precious water were held sacred at this great Mayan–Toltec centre – Chichen Itzá translates as 'at the mouth of the well of the Itzá'. Cenotes also acted as Xibalba – portals to another realm – and they housed important gods. Of the two surviving cenotes, one was held in such esteem that it prompted precious votive offerings. For the Maya, the domain of spirituality flowed above and beyond the earth; they mapped the heavens and tracked celestial bodies as they sought to understand the cosmos.

Extant structures include the Temple of the Warriors, the Temple of Kukulkan, El Caracol, the Ball Court, and the Temple of the Jaguars. Each had a specific function, proclaimed by the artists whose skills adorn them and, as with many cultures, activity and belief were mutually sustaining. For example, the pyramidal Temple of Kukulkan, sacred to the feathered serpent god of the same name, embodies a huge calendar. Steps on each of the four sides number the days between the year's major solar junctures. A shared top step brings the total to the number of days per year. At the time of equinox the stairs throw a snaking line of shadows down the pyramid, animating a huge sculpted serpent head waiting at the ground, thus announcing the change of season.

The Ball Court allowed communion with the gods and ensured balance between divergent forces, such as night and day. Within the Ball Court, the Game, a profound religious rite, was performed. It involved seven players per team, a goal was placed seven units high and a shout in the middle of the court bounced around in seven echoes. Multiply that number by 13 (the steps a Mayan needed to go through to reach heaven) and you will know the number of stairs on each face of the Temple of Kukulkan. Ideas resound through time and space at Chichen Itzá.

previous pages Soaring over 24 metres (78 feet), the Temple of Kukulkan, or El Castillo, represents the nine planes of the underworld. Each face of the pyramid has 92 steps leading up to the temple, which holds carvings of gods, priests and warriors. Within this great edifice is a smaller pyramid containing yet another temple that houses a red throne in the shape of a jaguar with jade eyes.

right From the top of El Castillo you can look down onto the Temple of Warriors, named for the hundreds of warriors carved in bas-relief on the columns in front and to the side. It is thought that these columns would have supported a thatched roof. Carved feathered serpents guard the stairs leading to the top of the temple.

right At Chichen Itzá beauty rubs shoulders with the gruesome reality of violent death. The Tzompantli, or Wall of Skulls, marks the place at which the heads of sacrificial victims were exhibited. Notice how no two are identical and all face in the same direction. Heart-eating eagles, snakes, warriors and feathered serpents can also be seen. These motifs are repeated elsewhere.

left At the entrance to the Temple of the Warriors a Chac Mool altar supports a tray that may have held sacrificial offerings. Chac Mool may have been a messenger between man and the gods and here the altar is flanked by two columnar, feathered serpents that represent Kukulkan.

Teotihuacán State of México, Mexico

Two vast pyramids and the Temple of the Feathered Serpent dominate the geometric layout of hundreds of buildings in the sacred city of Teotihuacán. This was a major religious centre, erected between the first and seventh centuries AD. At its peak it was one of the largest cities in the world with a population of over 100,000. No one knows why the city was abandoned in the seventh century, but when the Aztecs came here about six centuries later they found ruins. However, they were overwhelmed by the powerful force of the place and, divining that it must be the birthplace of the gods, named it 'Teotihuacán', meaning 'Place of the Gods' in the Aztec Nahuatl tongue.

The feathered serpent god, known here as Quetzalcoatl, is honoured with a temple, which it is thought was used to mark time over the 260-day calendar. There was a feathered serpent head for each of these days, which in turn would be marked to count the passing of time. The god's name comes from the conjoined words, *quetzal*, meaning precious feather, and *coatl*, meaning snake. The serpent form represents earthly fertility and the long green quetzal feathers are scarce, precious and beautiful.

But why was the city built here and why did it come to have such religious gravity? The Pyramid of the Sun may hold the answer. Beneath it a four-chambered cave has been discovered. To early Mesoamericans, caves bore deep significance. They were womb-like and points of arrival for the gods; they housed the ancestors and were gates to the beyond. Having four chambers, this particular cave represented the four corners of the cosmos and so its power was magnified. Little wonder then that people settled here, began farming and building above and around this powerhouse, the fount of time and creation.

right Strong sunlight throws crisp shadow and light onto the tiers of the pyramids, lending authority to these bold, assertive structures. Originally, only the priests and dignitaries would have had access to the stairs and platforms, as they were reserved for ceremonial purposes. Today, tourists have the privilege of being able to climb to the top, taking their time to absorb the atmosphere of this extraordinary place under its massive sky.

far left In the middle of the city is the Ciudadela, a plaza of about 160,000 square metres (525,000 square feet), which was probably an arena for ritual performance. The stairs of the main pyramid chime to a unique acoustic performance of their own. They echo with a sound that mimics the call of the Quetzal bird, which lends its name to Quetzalcoatl, the feathered serpent god associated with Venus.

centre Many murals adorn the walls of Teotihuacán's great buildings. Local pigments were used, such as the sparkling specular hematite. Red symbolized blood and immortality; black, death and solemnity. While we don't know what sounds scroll from the mouths of the figures we can see that they seem to inhabit the same plane as the butterflies, which may represent the afterlife.

left Carvings such as this would have originally been highly coloured and some traces of pigment still cling within the shelter of the deeper contours. It is thought that this may represent the jaguar aspect of Tlaloc – god of rain, floods and drought. The Palace of the Jaguar is one of the smaller pyramids, thought to have been built to house the high priests.

Serpent Mound

Ohio Brush Creek, Ohio, USA

The Serpent Mound is a sinuous line of raised earth with a coiled tail, seven loops and an ovoid head. At 405 metres (1,329 feet) long, this is the largest known earthwork effigy. However, these simple facts belie the convoluted mystery that unfurls on encountering 'the snake'. Burials close by date from the Adena peoples (500 BC–200 AD) and they were long credited with its construction, though the purported dates for the underlying structure conflict with that evidence, adding to the site's mystery. Other researchers favour the Fort Ancient culture (900–1600 AD), but why it was made is another question. The serpent rests above the scar of a great cryptoexplosion – a meteoric, gaseous or volcanic eruption. We can only speculate as to why this spot was chosen – perhaps to heal the wound in the earth's crust or in response to the impact made in the local topography. The alignment has caused debate too, marking midsummer sunset and midwinter sunrise. However, those who attribute it to the Fort Ancient people would highlight the brilliant appearance of Halley's Comet in 1066, which caused wonder and fear in many cultures. It is tempting to think that the Serpent Mound was built to honour that potent dart of celestial light or even that from a supernova burning so strongly in 1070 that for two weeks it marked the sky by day and night.

right This enigmatic icon, the Serpent Mound, sits in a crater above a network of caves. Serpents have long been potent symbols, in ancient times representing wisdom, due in part to the venom's use in shamanic ritual. Repeated patterns such as loops and spirals were early art forms created to aid meditation and altered states of consciousness.

Grand Canyon National Park
Arizona, USA

For millions of years the Colorado River has been carving the Grand Canyon, exposing the earth's history in bands of vibrant strata and vertiginous sculpture. For at least 4,000 of those years, people have been working here too. Despite the harsh conditions, many tribes have thrived in this region, drawing strength from their religious beliefs and sacred lifestyles. They have been hunter-gatherers, farmers, weavers, wanderers and settlers. While the many tribes have intricate and distinct interpretations of the sacred, it is worth considering some of the common threads that breathe life and weave spirit through the Grand Canyon.

According to Hopi tradition, their ancestors the Hisatsinom emerged into the canyon through an underground cave and dwell there still. Machu, guardian of the world, formed an agreement with the Hopi that if they took the cloak of guardianship they might stay. So protection of the land is a sacred duty to them, its wellbeing their responsibility. The Navajo, also known as Diné, who came here perhaps 700 years ago, are also intricately bound to the idea of protecting creation. The Kachinas, ancestral spirits of the mountain, must not be offended by our despoiling the earth. Havasupai religion also insists its followers must be protectors of Grandmother Canyon as it is the birthplace of humankind and hosts creation's annual renewal. This then is a landscape deeply revered by those who inhabit it and who expect their spirits to rest here with those of their ancestors. Some outsiders would ignore tribal beliefs and the desire to stay faithful to sacred obligations, claiming the right to exploit the natural resources of the canyon for industry and leisure. While many tribes may welcome visitors, it is perhaps the spiritual tourists' sacred duty to respect the lifestyle of those who have a greater claim here than we do.

right The thrilling landscape of the canyon is breathtaking and wondrous, but just as light and shade go hand in hand, the counterpart of this astonishing beauty is danger. Lightning can reach for 16 kilometres (10 miles) and flash floods come from nowhere reinforcing the notion that nature has the upper hand and, as the native tribes have always known, must be respected.

above Marble Canyon marks the western boundary of the Navajo Nation and, at almost 2 kilometres (1¼ miles) is the narrowest part of the canyon, which twists and coils for 445 kilometres (277 miles). Data alerted authorities to the need for conservation plans, without which creatures such as the bald eagle and grey wolf might have become extinct. Thankfully, the canyon's National Park status safeguards the rare and endemic.

top Farming necessitates storage in times of plenty. The Nankoweap Granaries are larders made by the Anasazi people who built into caves with mud bricks. These could be seen as analogous to the underground chambers from which the seeds of life burst forth. Also left in caves by the Desert Culture were split-twig figurines of animals, indicating rituals asking blessings on the hunt.

right Early peoples left artefacts along the canyon that show human activity here reaching back 12,000 years. However, only a fraction of it has been extensively examined, raising the prospect of untold secrets. The sense of power, mystery and our emergence from the dust is almost palpable. Natural processes alter the landscape but the spirit you can sense here is indestructible.

Wrangell–Saint Elias National Park and Preserve
Alaska, USA

On both sides of the border between Canada and Alaska is a hugely diverse landscape of mountains, coastline and the world's largest non-polar ice-field. The delicate ecosystems and endangered species inhabit one of the largest protected areas on earth. Black and grizzly bears live here along with moose and caribou, eagles and salmon. In these times of climate change all of this seems ever more precious as the glacier acquires the transient fragility of the wildflower. This highlights the wilderness as a sacred gift and our need to tread lightly.

The human population in this area is low, but as people have lived here for thousands of years there are plenty with

deep, cultural roots. They understand the spirit of the place; it infuses their blood. To the Tlingit and Chugach people, the natural world and all that grows and moves upon it is irrevocably interconnected. The age-old gods and spirits ruled the elements and dictated the movement of the creatures within the waters and upon the mountain. Then in turn, animals could be called upon by the shaman, who was priest, healer and guide. To the Tlingit, the vital source of life is within and can be equated to breath, while after death and cremation the soul reaches 'the other side' via the forest and mountain top. Natural dichotomies inform much of Tlingit belief so that every aspect of life has its

above Known as the 'mountain kingdom of North America', Wrangell–Saint Elias is named after two of its mountain ranges. While other cultures have built temples, pyramids and spires to echo the mountains, here there were originally no formal sites of worship. Spirituality was generated by the land and all it supported, nature having its own will, life-force and mystery.

counterpart. The forest with its dark and hidden dangers is in contrast to the open, flat surface of the sea, which provides so much food that 'when the tide goes out, the table is set'. The one has hidden forces while in the other, the forces are apparent.

above Bagley is one of the largest ice-fields in North America, its ice columns and bridges sparkling before the sun as it moves behind the mountain. Traditional Tlingit stories belong to the cultural system and although it is tempting to relate the 'Theft of Daylight' story here, seek out an official version of this and other delightful tales.

above Petroglyph Beach in Wrangell has over 40 carvings worked into stone. They show animals, people and patterns and may have served magical or religious purposes. The spiral is one of the oldest cosmic symbols, with its central point around which all else revolves. Still used as an aid to meditation, the spiral may be the root from which labyrinths grew.

above Icebergs break away from the Nizina Glacier to float into the lake and feed the river. The still-melt waters of the lake are gracefully surrounded with the presence of translucent icebergs and the river slips away through mountainous landscape to join the Chitina and Copper rivers in an extensive delta ecosystem bursting with salmon and other precious natural gifts.

Niagara Falls

Ontario, Canada, and New York, USA

In *American Notes*, Charles Dickens wrote that Niagara Falls made him feel 'near to my Creator… Peace of Mind, tranquillity, calm, recollections of the Dead, great thoughts of Eternal Rest and Happiness… '. The Iroquois Indians knew the Falls to be sacred, for Manitou, Creator and Lifegiver, dwelt there. This was where the good spirits of the dead could rise with the Falls' vapours on their way to the Happy Hunting Ground, with bad souls tumbling for eternity into the turbulence.

One of the most famous tales associated with the Falls, and it has many versions, is that of Lelawala, Maid of the Mist. Her tribe, the Ongiaras, were falling to an unknown illness. They tried to placate the Thunder God, Hinum, by sending gifts over the waterfalls, but the dying continued. To increase the value of the sacrifice it was decided that Lelawala should be given. She bravely stepped into the canoe but was caught mid-fall by Hinum's two sons, desirous of her beauty. She promised to accept the one who could explain the deaths. The youngest told her of a serpent poisoning the water so that he could devour the dead. Lelawala's spirit passed this news to the braves of her tribe who overcame the serpent. The body of the dying serpent formed the semicircle brink of the Horseshoe Falls and Lelawala lives on in the rising vapours as the Maid of the Mists.

left and below The astonishingly vital beauty of the Niagara Falls is powerfully moving – visually, aurally and emotionally. Naturally occurring negative ions, found in mountains and at the coast, are formed here by the pounding of water. These have an uplifting, energizing effect, leading to heightened awareness. This has always contributed to the notion of waterfalls having a life-enhancing presence.

europe

The dominant faiths practised in Europe today are Christianity, Islam and Judaism, and although Europe has the western world's highest atheist and agnostic numbers, pilgrimage is on the increase. Pilgrimage involves a journey and an end point, each of which has a spiritual and usually a communal dimension, whether it be to ask for healing, forgiveness or guidance. Within Europe the activity began in the fourth century, around the Mediterranean, and fanned out across the continent, accompanied by increased trade and prosperity for the destination and respite points along the way.

The natural environment plays a role in forming cultural development, just as the creative works of humankind are inevitably imprinted upon the landscape and the elements that inspired them. The Thingvellir National Park, shown here, is a good example of that sacred relationship.

In this chapter we visit several pilgrim sites, some of which tell of historical individuals, the saints of early Christianity, their journeys and the steely determination needed to imprint their nascent faith into mainstream culture. But long before the saints were born, in early times, there were polytheist religions in Europe, with people worshipping in groves, by water sources and at other natural features such as those in Iceland, around the numinous landscape of Thingvellir National Park.

When early sacred sites were marked, it was by those whose names we shall never know. They etched their beliefs, hopes and fears into the stuff of landscape. For example at Lascaux 17,000 years ago, artists were using coloured earth and charcoal to bring the outside world of animals and hunting into the depths of womb-like caves, wherein they made contact with the spirit world through ritual acts, including painting. They honed an inner sanctum through which they could pass to another realm, one that touched the ineffable. Sheltered from rain and erosion, their galleries have been brought safely to a world undreamed of by their makers. Animals were depicted by artists around the Alta Fjord in Norway, too. Here they were gouged into stone, not tucked away in caves but running through the open. Exposed to the elements they were engraved by sharpened point, their movements lacking the fluidity and dynamism caught by

Lascaux's artists, but like the cave paintings, the creatures and the acts depicted lie at the heart of the cultural interdependence between spiritual and physical existence. Also prancing through the open is the magnificent White Horse at Uffington in England. It too is cut into the surface that holds it, deeply and on a scale so large as to be unreadable at close hand, where visual integrity is confounded, though its sinuous lines are an abstracted joy.

And animals feature in the mind when considering Saint Francis of Assisi. It was he who preached to the beasts of air and field, and having eschewed worldly comforts he turned towards the poverty and humility that is also associated with Saint Patrick in Ireland and Saint Ninian in Scotland. Both studied at the monastery of Martin of Tours in France and both left there fired with the desire to preach Christianity. The places we identify with these saints are still ones of pilgrimage, as is Canterbury Cathedral, with its saintly connections, extraordinary events and stories.

However it is Glastonbury that claims Great Britain's earliest Christian connection, for it is said that as a child, Christ himself came here with Joseph of Arimathea. Glastonbury is an area humming with a wide spectrum of spiritual activity, from the prehistoric to the New Age. Like so many ancient sites of spiritual significance, Glastonbury's change of use has led

to a shift in geographical and religious focus. Whereas at Castlerigg stone circle in Cumbria, the core of sacred activity is held within one field, and all of the stones can be touched within a short space of time. The small arena contained within this mysterious ring echoes the surrounding hills, and the monoliths are placed to mark the heavenly bodies and embed their powers into early culture. This is somewhat similar to the purpose of the standing stones at Carnac in France, though that site is huge, and some of the stones are too.

Not very far away at Chartres Cathedral early astronomy was adopted and absorbed by Christianity, and signs of the zodiac have been incorporated into glass and stone as indicators of seasonal activities. Chartres was built upon a site long revered for its sacred waters, and sacred waters are what draws so many people to Lourdes for healing and for pilgrimage, following an apparition of the Virgin Mary. Also in France, the steep steps to the Church of Notre Dame in Rocamadour can be climbed. A place of miracles and a pilgrimage destination in its own right, this is also one of the possible starting points for the Way of Saint James pilgrimage, which leads to the cathedral at Santiago de Compostela, the Field of Stars, across the Pyrenees in Spain. Many aim to end their journey here on Saint James' day, he being patron saint of apothecaries and pharmacists. This is

something Saint James holds in common with Apollo, the Greek god of medicine and healing, who is closely associated with Delphi, a mysterious early pilgrim site high on the side of Mount Parnassus. Mount Athos, the second Greek site in this chapter, was once dedicated to the ancient gods, too, with a temple devoted to Apollo. But over time the ancient gods gave way to Christianity, following a visit from the Virgin Mary, and Mount Athos is now an Orthodox monastic community. It was from here that monks left the warm sunshine and made for chilly northwest Russia and the Monastery of the Transfiguration at Valaam, where succour and a resolute creative spirit have risen above repeated struggles, and the site has become a place of healing, forgiveness and guidance. Visiting these places in the labyrinthine manner mentioned above would clearly be impractical, though following those connections illustrates just some of the links and common ground covered by the realm of sacredness and those in search of the ineffable.

left to right Glastonbury Tor, Glastonbury, Somerset, England; White Horse at Uffington, Oxfordshire, England; Sami Rocks, Alta Fjord, Finnmark, Norway; the Basilica of San Francesco d'Assisi, Umbria, Italy.

Glastonbury Tor
Glastonbury, Somerset, England

The town of Glastonbury is a multifaceted place, full of legend, speculation and history. For many centuries visitors and pilgrims have been drawn to the Tor, the abbey, the holy wells and Wearyall Hill. To understand its magnetism it is necessary to learn how the area came to be so revered over the years.

Glastonbury was originally an island amid wetland. The area has been inhabited since prehistoric times; around 300–200 BC it was a Celtic lake village. Over time the land level rose and the area was drained, creating the plain that is now known as the Somerset Levels. Climbing 158 metres (518 feet) above this flat expanse is Glastonbury Tor, a teardrop-shaped hill that was formed by slow, aqueous erosion. Centuries ago, amid this marshy, misty land, this remarkable formation would have been a visual focus that inevitably led to spiritual speculation. The Tor shows signs of pre-Christian religious activity, perhaps centring on the swollen belly of the Earth Goddess. Its sides have been terraced, forming what many believe to be an ancient labyrinth or processional route. This would make sense; if the top of the mound had been a place for ceremony, then it would have needed a dignified and meaningful approach. One old name that was used for the tor was Ynys-witrin (Island of Glass), but it is from Celtic legend that Avalon, from Ynys yr Afalon (after the Celtic god Avallach), comes. Beyond the Tor it is said that the boy Jesus visited and built a church with Joseph of Arimathea. After Christ's death Joseph returned and as he landed drove his staff into the ground on Wearyall Hill. There it took root and became the sacred Glastonbury Thorn. Descendants of the tree are said to still grow to this day, flowering at Christmas.

With the Gospel, Joseph also brought the Holy Grail, from which Jesus drank at the Last Supper. He supposedly hid it at the foot of the Tor and from the site water sprang forth, bringing health and strength to those who drank. This spring is now called the Chalice Well and it is possible that this story is the source of the tales of King Arthur and his quest for the Holy Grail.

Today, Glastonbury draws pilgrims from many traditions – Christians, pagans, Holy Grail seekers and even music lovers for the now-famous music festival. The town itself is flooded with a sparkling sea of 'New Age' shops, with the Tor, the Abbey and Wearyall Hill continuing to rise, with a timeless significance, behind them.

Stonehenge
Wiltshire, England

Presiding over the landscape of Salisbury Plain, Stonehenge inspires awe, imagination and endless questions. For the more that is discovered about the place, the more our understanding becomes enmeshed in conflicting opinion. Discoveries send research in new directions with academics, archaeologists and spiritual seekers often recognizing different truths. And despite the apparent wealth of evidence that has come to light, only a fraction of the surrounding landscape has been studied, so theories will continue to shift and turn as time reveals more.

However, some aspects are agreed upon. Like the iconic trilithons, the erection of the site was in three parts, spanning the period 3100 to 1100 BC. Although it is not the world's largest stone circle, it is the only one with lintels along the top. And no one doubts that the sophisticated engineering and the mass of the stones in their concentric arrangement all add up to a phenomenal achievement. There also seems to be a tacit agreement that the total is worth more than the sum of its parts, even though we do not yet know what those all those parts may prove to be!

A common question is whether there is something inherently significant about the positioning of Stonehenge or if it was built here for purely practical reasons. Dowsing reveals multiple ley lines intersecting within the henge, suggesting that the site is a hub of energy, perhaps better understood and harnessed by the ancients than by today's cultures. It is now known that the pattern of the stones' arrangement was plotted with cord and pegs and fits tightly and precisely within a geometry, beautiful in its simplicity, but which had eluded modern minds until very recently. Thus connections exist beneath the monument and they radiate across the landscape meeting many other sacred sites in the region.

But Stonehenge also makes connections way above Salisbury Plain. If the stones' arrangement conforms to elements on and in the earth, it also extends to the heavens. Alignment to the summer solstice is the annual event that attracts most fervent celebration. And early use as an astronomical observatory is another mooted function, tracking starlight that has travelled for far longer even than the stones have stood here.

left Soft light gives a gentle glow to the stones and the atmosphere lends a subtle palette. Stonehenge has always inspired legend, folklore, art and literature, enriching our cultural heritage beyond measure. Archaeological finds show that travellers visited from way beyond England. We may never know what they sought and found but seeking and wondering are a potent source of creativity.

right This aerial view of Stonehenge gives a clear indication of its relationship to Salisbury Plain and allows us to imagine how the rings must have looked when complete. A concrete replica and computer-generated data suggest that the site would have had vibrant acoustic qualities, making music and voices sound incredibly resonant; a powerful aid to ceremony.

White Horse at Uffington
Oxfordshire, England

This stylized horse, in Uffington, Oxfordshire, is Britain's most elegant and oldest hill figure. It is fashioned from deep trenches cut into the hillside. The trenches are packed with white chalk so that the figure stands out across the vale that bears its name. Tests have revealed that the substance at the bottom of the trenches dates back at least 2,600 years, possibly longer, making the horse approximately 3,000 years old.

The remarkable landscape that surrounds the figure was vertically folded and pleated by the forces of the last ice age. At the foot of these creases is a curious flat-topped mound, known as Dragon Hill. Tradition tells that Saint George defeated

left This extraordinary landscape was carved by the last Ice Age. The near vertical folds in the hill side lead down to a flat valley bottom called The Manger. This is because on moonlit nights, the White Horse descends from the hill to feed here. It is also a spot beloved by artists as the abstract forms symbolise the other- worldly atmosphere and trigger the imagination.

below The magical elements of this wonderful landscape are captured here. Uffington Castle is outlined by the earthworks with the White Horse and Dragon Hill close to the centre of the picture. The Manger is the flat valley skirted by the glacier-carved folds to the left. To the bottom of the picture the ancient trading route known as The Ridgeway links many places of mystery.

below The White Horse runs 110 metres (360 feet) across the hillside yet despite its size is difficult to read from close proximity, as the lines become abstracted as you approach. An aerial view offers the clearest view, leading to the idea that the creature may have been made to be seen by Epona, the Celtic Lunar goddess and protector of horses.

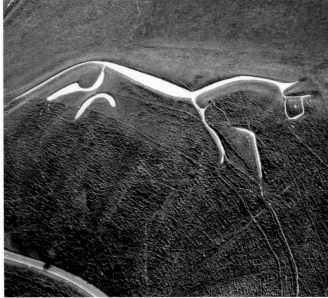

the dragon on top of this hill and its blood poisoned the grass so that it remains bare to this day. The figure on the hillside is commonly thought to represent his steed, or even the dragon itself. The horse is positioned on the hillside to the east of the folds and faces the setting sun. Above it are more folds in the landscape – this is an Iron Age hill fort, created during the seventh century BC and now called Uffington Castle. Some myths suggest that the 110-metre (361-feet) long figure is a Saxon victory sign marking the defeat of the Danes by Alfred the Great in the year 890 AD. If the horse does predate the fort, then it may have been adopted by those who lived there.

The figure's full glory is best appreciated from afar, above even, suggesting that it may have been made to be seen from the heavens. Perhaps it was drawn to placate Epona, the Celtic lunar goddess of fertility, healing and the protector of horses. It is said that on moonlit nights the figure leaves its hillside to feed in the Manger, the flat valley bottom. .

Over the centuries, the horse has been protected by local people who held religious scouring ceremonies to maintain the sinuous lines and the brightness of the white chalk. These ceremonies later evolved into days of festivity and today the horse draws many visitors, including artists, archaeologists and ley line readers.

Castlerigg Stone Circle

Keswick, Cumbria, England

Known locally as Druid's Circle and the Keswick Carles, this circle dates from around 3200–3000 BC and is one of the earliest stone circles in Britain. The magnificence of the site comes not from the actual stones – the tallest stone is only 2.3 metres (7½ feet) in height – but from the setting. This wondrous place is 213 metres (700 feet) above sea level and set within a stunning sweep of shifting light and fickle weather. Standing within the circle you find yourself surrounded not only by the stones, but also by Skiddaw, Blencathra, Lonscale Fell, Low Rigg, High Rigg, Cat Bells and Derwent Fells. These hills shape the landscape of the area and the stones echo their form. They sit so comfortably within their setting because the landscape spawned the circle, and the circle echoes the landscape. There is a harmony of the genius locus here.

Thirty-eight stones, made of local metamorphic slate, form a slightly elliptical ring, 30 metres (98½ feet) across. Within the ring there are a further ten stones. Two tall pillars mark the entrance and inside there are three small cairns (a heap of stones piled up as a memorial), suggesting that this may have been a place for the dead. Traces of charcoal have been found in this area, which proves that fires had been lit at some point. It is thought that this ring was a Neolithic and Bronze Age meeting place – circular enclosures such as this were usually a forum for ceremony, ritual and worship – and the natural theatre here is certainly highly conducive to such activities.

The static features of this site come to life and take on a particular dynamism when the place is observed over time. For example, the midwinter sunset throws a shaft of light onto the Bun Stone in the cove, and other stones are similarly positioned to mark significant points in the solar and lunar calendars. The midsummer sunset, the most northerly and most southerly moonset, the most southerly moonrise, midwinter moonrise and midwinter sunrise are all marked out by the placing of the stones, indicating a society for whom seasons and cycles held deep significance. Changing light and the night sky contribute their own timeless magic here.

Today, people still talk in terms of the stones having 'active' and 'resting' phases and there is anecdotal evidence supporting this activity. During 1919 Mr T. Singleton and his companion watched as globes of white light moved among the stones. In more recent times a self-confessed sceptic was taken aback by the humming noise emanating from the ring as his wife touched and counted each stone in turn. Some visitors claim the stones can cure headaches, while others find solutions to problems here.

Castlerigg is a place that offers visitors what they want to find. It is a place to contemplate nature, wonder at the wisdom of those who have gone before and the knowledge lost, a resting place to recharge walkers' energy and a source of inspiration for writers, poets and painters. Summer solstice attracts musicians, fire jugglers, wiccans (members of Neopagan religion) and locals who come to enjoy and absorb the essence of this mysterious site.

left The light, and the shadows it brings, are crucial to understanding the function of Castlerigg; in fact, Professor Alexander Thom called the place 'an astronomical observatory'. Imagine how the passing sun swings shadows around the ring, stretching and shrinking the stones as it travels. Note too the ridges in the field around the circle.

left Known locally as the Druids' Circle, another name for the formation is the Keswick Carles, and this comes from a legend telling that the stones are actually petrified people. The fells around the area are said to resonate with the sound of enigmatic music from time to time and the ring itself has been the site of other supernatural phenomena.

right The shapes within Castlerigg circle echo the forms of the surrounding landscape. This scene also shows the mysterious cove, known as the Sanctuary, which is unique to Castlerigg. Its exact function is unknown but charcoal traces have been found within. At midwinter, alternating sunset shadows appear to focus light onto the Bun Stone.

right below Never fully excavated, the site may have been a trading place for stone axes and other artefacts, but it is the arcane and numinous qualities of Castlerigg that fascinate most enduringly. This is a place where the natural and the manmade elements work in complete harmony.

Canterbury Cathedral
Canterbury, Kent, England

As the seat of the Archbishop of Canterbury, the cathedral is a focal point for the worldwide community of Anglican Christians. Saint Augustine, as the first Archbishop of Canterbury, is the man usually associated with bringing Christianity to these islands but, in fact, nearby Saint Martin's Church predates his arrival in 597. Augustine had been given the mission of converting England to Christianity by Pope Gregory the Great, who thought the Angles he had seen looked like 'not Angles but Angels' and so ought to be won over. On arriving in Canterbury, Augustine and his fellow monks were given a church by King Ethelbert, whose Queen was already a Christian. Augustine very soon established a community here which, by 998, was living according to the Rule of Saint Benedict and did so until the Dissolution in 1540.

Over the centuries the cathedral has been shaped by many other significant saints and archbishops – Honorus, Theodore, Odo, Dunstan, Alphege, Anselm, Thomas,

far left Bursts of coloured light spill into the space like fresh paint, but this image of Thomas à Becket shows only a fraction of the wonderful collection of stained glass at Canterbury. During the twelfth century craftsmen from France and England co-operated over several decades to tell stories from the Bible and of the lives of the saints in a form that delights the senses.

centre There are twenty-one bells at Canterbury Cathedral: fourteen ringing bells in the Oxford Tower, six to chime the time in the Arundel Tower, and in the Bell Harry Tower, shown here, Bell Harry acts as the 'passing Bell' to mark the loss of a sovereign or Archbishop.

left Built in the perpendicular style the nave was completed in 1405; its forest of towering perpendicular columns lifts the spirit heavenwards. The word 'nave' comes from the Latin *navis*, or ship, because of the shape, and perhaps refers to Noah's Ark. In Christian art a ship often symbolizes the church.

Edmund and Thomas Cranmer – their special gifts adding to the accumulation of prayers laid down by ordinary pilgrims and worshippers. However, the figure who has stayed most vividly in the public imagination is Saint Thomas à Becket. On a chilly winter morning during 1170, at an altar in the cathedral, he was murdered by four knights hoping to ingratiate themselves with King Henry II. Henry had expressed a wish to be rid of 'this turbulent priest', a comment misinterpreted by the knights as a command.

On becoming Archbishop, Thomas had sought to purify the church, taking a strong and apparently turbulent role, whereas the King had hoped that Thomas would be a malleable ally. Eventually Henry was threatened with excommunication,

leading to his outburst and the knights' heinous deed. There was public outcry at this murder of a holy man on holy ground. On the very night of his murder, miracles began happening in such numbers that two monks were set the task of recording them and multitudes of pilgrims followed. Three years later, Thomas was declared a martyr by Pope Alexander and by the fourteenth century Canterbury had become the most proclaimed of all pilgrimage places. Nevertheless, violence and destruction returned; Thomas's shrine was smashed by King Henry VIII in 1538, puritans sacked the place in 1642 and fire struck twice. Yet faith and devotion have endured, as they have in so many troubled holy places.

Saint Ninian's Cave and White House

Isle of Whithorn, Dumfries and Galloway, Scotland

Saint Ninian was the first to bring Christianity to Scotland. It was from him that Bede tells us 'the southern Picts received the true faith by the preaching of Bishop Ninias, a most reverend and holy man of the British nation'. Whithorn takes its name from the whitewashed chapel that he built and called Candida Casa, or White House, which was translated by local tribes as 'Hwit Aerne', hence the name Whithorn.

Ninian was born around 360 and as a young man was moved to serve Christ in his native Galloway. Thirsting for knowledge and learning, he made an astonishing decision and walked to Rome, receiving education from the Pope and also the support he needed to fulfill his vocation. He returned to Scotland via France, where he spent time with, and gained encouragement from, Saint Martin of Tours.

On returning home, Ninian, now a bishop, began his ministry by preaching a gentle faith of tolerance and love among the Britons and the Picts. While he and some of the monks who came with him were building the chapel, word came of the death of Saint Martin and so the building was dedicated in his name, the whitewashed walls marking it as a site of significance within the landscape. In 397, with a strong foothold in the local community, Ninian built Whithorn Priory, the first in Britain. As his teaching spread, Ninian

above left Saint Ninian's Chapel was, and still is, used by pilgrims on the route to Whithorn. It would be tempting to think that it stands on the site of his original Candida Casa but that is more likely to be inland, beneath the Priory. However, for many this isolated spot is the spiritual focus of the Isle of Whithorn.

above The approach to Saint Ninian's Cave may well be deserted when you visit and the shingle shore holds no footprints. All the same, you will feel the presence of those who have been before and find the marks they have left in the form of carvings, driftwood crosses and a mound of prayer stones.

became known for his miracles, including restoring sight to a tribal chieftain, which in turn led to many converting to Christianity. A missionary and evangelist, Ninian was responsible for bringing Christian spirituality and the Gospel to a broad swathe of Britain. Through his travels and training, he connected these bleak and windswept parts to Europe's Christian movement and such was the respect for him that a cathedral was built to house his shrine.

A few miles away from the Priory is a dramatic stretch of coastline and there, up a little slope and just a few yards from the high-tide line, is a small cave. It is to here that Saint Ninian withdrew when in need of solitude for contemplation and respite.

From inside the cave, darkness frames the shore and sea with a jagged blackness so that, by contrast, the outside world looks brighter and more focused. Although the shingle shore holds no footprints, it is known that pilgrims have been coming to Saint Ninian's cave for many hundreds of years, leaving carvings of crosses and other symbols on the cave walls. At the mouth of the cave there is a heap of stones. It is traditional here to seek out a pebble crossed with white silica and leave it at the mouth of the cave with a prayer. There are also crosses made of driftwood and bound with seaweed. Even if you are the only person there, you will certainly feel the presence of others who have been before.

right and far right History, anecdote, and archaeology weave a complex story around Whithorn Priory. Evidence points to this being the site of the White House, but overlapping footprints from further buildings over hundreds of years mark a site where mystery may be better savoured intact than unravelled. The cemetery is the location of the Golgotha Stone, an eighth-century grave slab marked by three crosses, which represent Christ's crucifixion between two thieves. Other stones from as early as 450 AD are also found here, and the variety and complexity of some of the patterning illustrate a strong sense of design and visual literacy among the craftsmen.

Croagh Patrick

Westport, County Mayo, Republic of Ireland

Known locally in County Mayo as the Reek and in early times as the Eagle Mountain, Croagh Patrick is a conical mountain with a footprint occupying an area 5 by 3 kilometres (8 by 5 miles) and a summit that reaches 762 metres (2,500 feet) above sea level.

Traces left by early people tell that this has been treated as a special place for at least 6,000 years. Perhaps they first came to honour the freshets of holy waters springing in from the mountainside with traces of gold. Then they felt the confluence of powerful forces – height, transient light and views to a sea strewn with islands. Next they stayed to use the soapstone and quartz, bury their dead, to stand stones in alignment to the solar calendar and wonder at the 'rolling sun' effect during the months we call April and July. Neolithic hunters were followed by Bronze Age settlers and aerial photography highlights their ancient hill fort, hut circles and a later monastic complex on the summit of the ridge.

The individual most identified with the mountain since the fifth century is Saint Patrick. Born in Scotland of high-ranking Roman parents during 387, Patrick was captured and taken as a slave to Ireland. There he served a cruel Druid master but learned the Celtic idiom and found himself moving closer to God. Encouraged by an angel, Patrick fled to France, coming under the influence of Saint Martin of Tours, among others. But he felt drawn back to Ireland and occasionally felt the folk he had met there pleading 'O holy youth, come back to Erin, and walk once more among us'.

right The tradition of pilgrimage to this holy mountain stretches back over 5,000 years from the Stone Age to the present day without interruption. Croagh Patrick is renowned for its Patrician Pilgrimage in honour of Saint Patrick, Ireland's patron saint. It was on the summit of the mountain that Saint Patrick fasted for forty days in 441 AD and the custom has been faithfully handed down from generation to generation.

Thingvellir National Park
Bláskógabyggo, Iceland

Famous for narrating its history in sagas, Iceland has many layers of social and natural expression. In this landscape of extremes the ground is a palimpsest of agriculture scribed over nature, erased and worked again, encoding the tale of Icelandic culture. Just as the ground records human progress, the ecosystem of Lake Thingvallavatn has been described as a perfect model of species evolution. This is a place at one with the richness of its past and with an eye to its future. For many people, being in the presence of nature is a magical and often teleological experience. It is not surprising then, that this phenomenal volcanic landscape of hot springs, icy waters and sparkling cascades by day, crowned with the aurora borealis at night, inspired its people to gather, talk and plan.

The name 'Thingvellir' means 'Parliament Plains' and describes exactly the use to which Icelanders put a part of this wondrous place. For here, in the year 930, the world's first parliament, or Althing, was established. Once a year representatives of the population would congregate to hear the Law Speakers pronouncing from the Law Rock. This was where decisions were made, laws disseminated and disputes settled right up until 1798. For example, in 997 trouble broke out when a Saxon priest named Thangbrand was sent by King Olaf Trygvason of Norway to bring Christianity to Iceland and quash the pagan gods. The dispute continued until the year 1000 when the pagan Law Speaker Thorgeir was made responsible for deciding the spiritual direction of the nation: should Icelanders continue to worship traditional pagan gods or turn to Christianity? After withdrawing for a night and a day, Thorgeir declared that Christianity was the way forward but paganism could continue, if practiced covertly! He later flung his wooden idols into a waterfall, which is still called 'Godafoss', or 'Waterfall of the Gods'. Today the sagas are regarded as a literary treasure and Thingvellir as a jewel.

right One of Iceland's most spectacular waterfalls, Godafoss is the Waterfall of the Gods into which Thorgeir flung his images of Norse gods, once he had embraced Christianity. A window in the cathedral at Akureyri narrates this story. The waters roar down the 12-metre (40-foot) drop and span more than 30 metres (98 feet), the vapours rising into the crisp air.

left The geology and ecosystems of Thingvellir confirm the area as a unique and valuable natural wonder. Lake Thingvallavatn has been described as being exemplary of species' evolution in nature and is Iceland's largest lake. It also has the distinction of being about 100 metres (328 feet) above sea level, yet at 114 metres (374 feet) is deep enough to reach below sea level.

above Thingvellir is one of Iceland's most popular tourists sites, with camping, angling, hiking and riding being just some of the activities enjoyed today. It is also visited for the reflective pursuits engendered by the area's natural phenomena and its transcendent, numinous beauty. The cultural history of the area is still unfolding.

Sami Rocks

Alta Fjord, Finnmark, Norway

More than 5,000 mysterious carvings lie scattered on the rocks at four sites around Alta Fjord, near the Arctic Circle in Norway. The main site, located at Jiepmaluokta about 4 kilometres (2½ miles) outside of Alta, contains around 3,000 individual carvings and has been turned into an open-air museum. Dating from around 4200–500 BC, the images were chiselled and scraped by artists within the hunting and fishing communities whose existence and spiritual life depended upon the creatures depicted. Along with elk and reindeer, bears and canines, there are geese and swans, salmon and whales. People are present too, with bows and arrows, fishing lines and boats, pregnant women and those giving birth. Musicians strike *runebommen*, the drum still used by Sami people in shamanic ritual.

Recently coloured to aid visibility, it is thought that originally the drawings were left unstained. If that is so, then how were they read? Gouging into stone is difficult, controlling a line takes skill. Scraping the surface would have left an easily made, transient line, but perhaps the sgraffito went beyond durability. Beneath an overhead sun, the unstained images melt invisibly into the stone. But at sunrise and dusk, when the sun is low or even at full moon, shadows spread, outlines clarify and figures reveal themselves. Emerging in the most magical light, the drawings would assume a powerful charge, and thus enjoy a sacred, arcane status.

And who were they made for? The drawings bear no clear orientation, no fixed viewpoint of up, down or ground. Does this

left, centre and above Petroglyphs are rock carvings and the term usually refers to prehistoric ones such as these around Alta Fjord. Now stained to facilitate interpretation, they were given to us by people we can never fully understand. The images do, however, add to our understanding of the activities and priorities of the ancient peoples who lived near the Arctic circle so long ago.

mean they were made to be seen from above and shared with the sky gods? The position of the drawings is significant too; the margins of land and sea are symbolic of changing realms, life-form and activity. They are borders regarded as the point at which the dead cross to another place. There is no doubt that the carvings were made to endure and to inspire; they continue to do both today.

Monastery of the Transfiguration
Island of Valaam, Russia

Lake Ladoga in northwest Russia stretches 219 kilometres (136 miles) north to south and is sprinkled with islands. Fifty of these form the Valaam archipelago, of which the Island of Valaam is the largest. It is also home to the Monastery of the Transfiguration and an astonishing range of flora and fauna. The sparkling waters are vibrant with aquatic life, including a unique subspecies of ringed seal. The varied shoreline gives way to forests ringing with birdsong, freshwater springs and fertile land.

Abundant natural beauty has always engendered worship and signs of early sacred ritual remain here. Monastic tradition tells that Saint Andrew came and destroyed the mountain altars dedicated to local spirit deities, replacing them with a stone cross, but there is no evidence for that. In fact, stories surrounding the early establishment of Christianity are conflicting as confusion was caused by repeated troubles such as plague, fire, invasion and raids, leading to the loss of records. However, Valaam has long been a place of spiritual focus for Russian Orthodoxy and the arrival of Saints Sergius and Herman is documented. They established the monastery in the tenth century and their ministry included miracles of healing and protection. The relics of these two holy men are preserved and celebrated to this day.

Just as Valaam's numinous natural beauty inspires worship and its isolation generates spiritual focus, those same qualities spark aesthetic creation. Abbot Damascene (1835–81) encouraged artists of many disciplines to visit. One of them, Tchaikovsky, found inspiration for his first symphony which he called 'Winter Dreams' in response to the experience of being snowed-in here. The alternating dissonance and harmony in the history of the monastery has stabilized and today there are about 200 residents who live to the rhythm of strict monastic routine balanced with creative and productive community life.

right Having undergone countless troubles in the past, the monastery is now thriving with a resident community offering hospitality to pilgrims. Drawing spiritual support from saints Sergius and Herman, the pilgrims cherish the wisdom dispensed by the brotherhood living here today, in a landscape conducive to reflection and devotional focus.

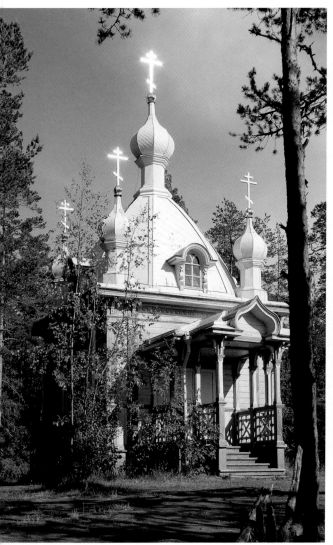

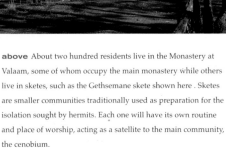

above About two hundred residents live in the Monastery at Valaam, some of whom occupy the main monastery while others live in sketes, such as the Gethsemane skete shown here . Sketes are smaller communities traditionally used as preparation for the isolation sought by hermits. Each one will have its own routine and place of worship, acting as a satellite to the main community, the cenobium.

above The skete of All Saints is the oldest monastic retreat in Valaam, and famous for its hermits, the elders Kleopa, Feodor and Leonid, and their disciples. Many of the skete's buildings were constructed in the mid 1840s, with the five-domed monastery seen here designed in 1846.

right The skete of Saint Nicholas the Wonder-Worker honours the patron saint of sailors and travellers. The elegant church was built in 1853 on the site of a former church and lighthouse. Several monks now live on this island linked, as if by stepping stones, to the larger community.

Lourdes
Lourdes, Midi-Pyrénées, France

Between February and July 1858, 14-year-old Bernadette Soubirous experienced 18 visions of a lady dressed in white, in a small grotto called Massabiele, close to her home on the banks of the River Gave de Pau. The figure told Bernadette that many people would come to this place and that the village priest should build a chapel there. The revelations continued and on the sixteenth visitation the figure declared herself to be 'The Immaculate Conception' – a term for the Virgin Mary unlikely to have reached Bernadette's ears before as it had only recently been defined in Rome. Another instruction was for the girl to wash herself in the spring, though no water was visible. She fell to the ground and dug with her hands until water sprang forth and gradually formed a pool. This was the sacred spring that so many people have now visited over the years.

Until this point there was no evidence of this area being particularly special; no standing stones, no prehistoric earth works and nothing in local lore. Yet it has become the largest healing shrine in Christendom. Originally the place was venerated for the

Virgin's appearances to Bernadette, but when powers of healing at that spot were noted towards the end of the nineteenth century it gained international repute. Miracles of healing have been authenticated and so the attraction continues to grow. Currently, four to six million pilgrims visit annually and to accommodate them the original pool has been channelled into other springs and baths. A basilica has been built over the site of the original spring and this too has been overwhelmed with visitors, leading to more chapels being added. Across the River Gave de Pau a hospice with 900 beds and yet more chapels have been built.

The healthy and the sick who visit Lourdes speak of finding encouragement, peace, hope, faith and healing. They bathe in the sacred waters, process with the Blessed Sacrament to the Shrine

above left Candles burn everywhere here in Lourdes, in chapels, in pavilions, by statues and springs. There are 22 places of worship, collectively known as the Sanctuaries. Countless pilgrims come here, individually and in groups.

above Images of the Virgin Mary are innumerable, and the Prayer to Our Lady of Lourdes runs to nearly 250 words. The gilded crown is symbolic of the reverence with which she is regarded.

and walk by candlelight with others, seeking personal or shared experiences. A site of such bustle, business and large crowds might seem like the last place a sick person would want or even have the strength to visit, yet Lourdes has the power to pull and support those who come. It may even be this faith and devotion that leaves an imprint that eventually magnifies the potency of the place.

above The Sanctuaries are open to visitors all year, with the main pilgrimage season running from the beginning of April to the end of October. Those who cannot make the journey may send for healing waters for use in their own homes, or request prayers to be said or candles to be lit for them by a 'feutier', one who supervises the use of candles here.

above The Virgin Mary appeared to Bernadette 18 times in all. In this image outside the Basilica of the Rosary at Lourdes, the young girl is using a rosary and supported by angels. We see the Virgin dressed according to Bernadette's description of the first apparition, all in white with a blue sash. Note how the earthly child is shown in humble stone while the heavenly beings are depicted in colourful mosaic.

right A detail of the architecture on the Basilica of the Rosary. Concentric arcs encircle the Virgin who sits within a mandorla – an oval halo. The dome above is surmounted by a golden crown, a cross and beyond that, the tallest spire. The figures on the balustrade give an indication of the scale of the building.

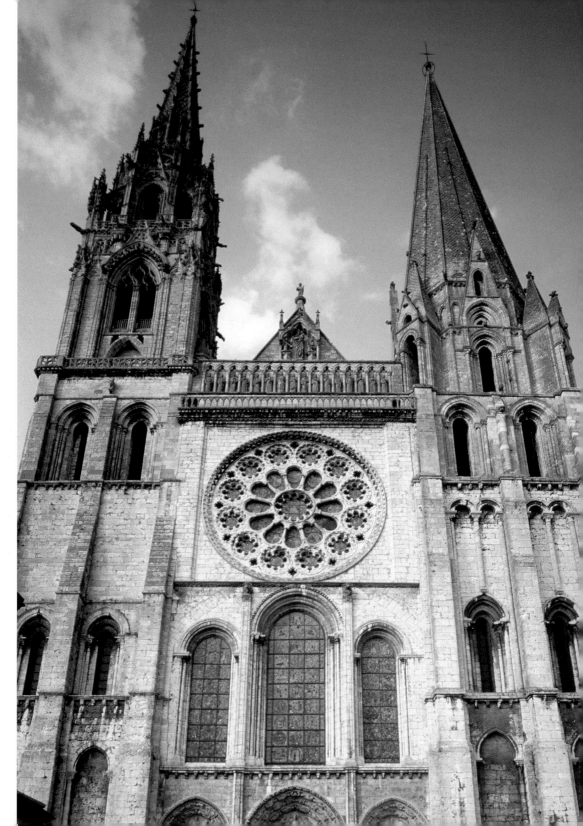

Notre Dame of Chartres

Chartres, Centre, France

This magnificent building is positioned on a site that was sacred well before Christianity arrived in France. Druids worshipped in the oak forests here and the spot has been a centre for worship and ritual ever since. Beneath the cathedral lies a well and a vault; tradition tells of an altar marking the spot and of a figure of a woman, seated with a child on her knee, bearing the legend 'the Virgin will give birth to a God'.

The cathedral that thousands visit today was begun in 1194, although the first church on the site was built around 67 AD, and Emperor Constantine erected the first cathedral here during the early fourth century. This cathedral was burned down by Hunaud, Duke of Aquitaine, and its replacement was destroyed by the Normans in 858. Yet more damage was inflicted by fires in 962 and in 1020, when it was totally destroyed. Work began on a new cathedral, which was consecrated in 1030, but fire struck again in 1194 leaving only the western section and two precious Marian relics – the figure in the crypt and the Veil of the Virgin.

The fact that this building exists today is thanks to the faith and determination of those who took on the responsibility and the huge tasks involved in planning, designing, refining and funding what is now known as Notre Dame of Chartres. From the outside, the two massive towers, one Early Gothic and one High Gothic, represent the prayers and souls of the worshippers reaching for heaven. Architecturally, the flying buttresses allow for larger windows that make the building feel as if it is lifting skywards. Although the full impact of the windows is felt from the inside, on a strongly lit day, the tracery and detail of the lanceate and rose windows promise delights upon entering, which is, of course, in parallel with the idea of entering heaven.

Inside the cathedral, huge pillars resemble the trees that once stood there, before the stone was quarried near Paris and floated in by water to build this incredible structure. More than 100 windows covering 3,150 square metres (33,906 square feet) combine in a meeting of colour, light, texture, pattern, narrative and instruction. At the west end a circular labyrinth dates from around 1230. A path of 12 rings turns through 28 loops that lead to the centre. The pilgrims would walk its 260-metre (853-feet) length, the twists and turns representing their path through life. Notre Dame of Chartres is still a place of worship and pilgrimage, and conservation and restoration continues – physical renewal confirming spiritual insistence.

above The north rose window with five lancets is called the Rose of France and dedicated to the Virgin Mary, Saint Anne and Blanche of Castille. Master glassmakers used their craft to superb ends and the 'blue of Chartres' is a term still used to this day. The twelve segments may reflect the influence of medieval astrology, which is also evident in the zodiac signs elsewhere in the building.

left This view of the west end shows the Jehan of Beauce tower (left) standing at 114 metres (377 feet) and the Romanesque tower (right) reaching 105 metres (349 feet) towards the heavens. There had been plans to erect five or six towers but complications and expenses kept the numbers down. The fine tracery of the rose window can been seen clearly from the outside, but inside, colour takes precedence as light shines through the glass.

above This detail of figures shows the skill of the craftsmen and the degree to which they understood form and solidity. The drapery hangs and folds, hands grasp objects and heads turn and look out to the world beyond. Although each figure is complete in his own right, notice how the rhythm of the workmanship unites them to make a convincing whole.

right The mid twelfth-century Royal Portal escaped the fire of 1194 and was incorporated into the reconstructed building. A monument of Early Gothic sculpture, the areas of sculptural decoration, including the tympanum, archivolts, lintel and jamb figures, constitute an integrated whole. Christ, placed in the centre within a mandorla of light, is flanked by the four beasts of the Apocalypse. On the lintel appear the 12 apostles and the single figures at either end are the Old Testament prophets Enoch and Elijah, noted for their prophecies of the Second Coming.

Cave of Lascaux
Montignac, Aquitaine, France

In 1940, in the Dordogne *département* of France, four boys exploring the banks of the River Vézère came across a tree that had been struck by lightning and uprooted, exposing a hole beneath. There they discovered a cavern, unknown even to local people. The space was found to house 600 paintings and 1,500 engravings of horses, bison and deer that had been made, over several generations, 17,190 years ago. With a culture that has long since gone, it is impossible to be sure exactly why certain things were done, but clearly this was not a place of casual graffiti. Abbe Breuil, a scientist and explorer and dubbed the 'Father of Prehistory', noted that although the caves were littered with tools and lamps, there was no sign of human inhabitation; here then was a place set aside for something special, sacred even.

A site such as this raises questions as to the nature of sacred space by virtue of the lack of information. There is no written or oral history here to confirm what people might like to believe.

above The Chinese Horse from the Painted Gallery is 1.5 metres (5 feet) long. The animal is outlined and shaded with charcoal and targeted by arrows. The artist has placed its hooves along a ridge on the wall, grounding it and so adding to the realism.

left A section of the frieze in the Painted Gallery. Here we see animals coming and going through a crevice in the ceiling, as though the activity continues out of sight and out of reach. As visibility here would be awkward, was this scene meant to be read while lying supine on the cave floor?

Some have suggested that these are trophy images. Others say it is a sympathetic hunting magic or shamanistic ritual asking for fertility within the 'womb' of the earth. If the artistic content is considered, the draftsmanship is hugely sympathetic to the context. Full use has been made of the contours of the cave to add three-dimensional form to the bulk of the beasts; they even run across the high ceilings. The observation is acute; the artists knew their subject and were fully engaged in expressing movement, power and speed. The pictures held a significance to those who drew them, beyond visual enjoyment – they belong to the realm of consciousness on some other level.

above Here we see a detail of one of the cows from the Painted Gallery ceiling, measuring 2.8 metres (9 feet) long. It has been found that the paintings are placed in areas of superior acoustic resonance. Imagine peering at these massive creatures while the striking of stones and shouts of your companions recreate the thundering of hooves.

above Is he dead, unconscious or in a trance? This figure shows a man with the beak of a bird (possibly a bird mask) and close to his hand a pole surmounted by a bird. Did flying creatures represent the flight of the soul into other realms of consciousness? Its also interesting to note the minimal treament of the man figure compared to the realistic treatment of the beast.

Church of Notre Dame

Rocamadour, Midi-Pyrénées, France

Zacchaeus was an unpopular tax collector of such small stature that to get a glimpse of Jesus he needed to climb a tree. Jesus noticed this gesture and, following a shared meal, Zacchaeus repented of his sinful lifestyle, restored fourfold the money he had taken from people and became a Christian. Some say he even became a servant in the household of the holy family. Subsequently, he was exiled from his homeland and tradition tells of how he came, by water, with his wife Veronica (who wiped Christ's face on his way to Calvary) to Aquitaine under the protection of an angel.

After Veronica's death he climbed to a spot 125 metres (410 feet) above the River Alzou in the ancient province of Quercy and became a hermit, building a chapel to honour the Virgin Mary. It is thought to be he who carved the Black Madonna with the Christ Child, which welcomes visitors to the Church of Notre Dame. Zacchaeus is now known as Saint Amadour – the name comes from *amator*, 'he who loves the rock'. Reports of miraculous events here drew the English King, Henry Plantagenet, King Saint Louis of France and Alphonse III of Portugal, and so the reputation of the site as a place of pilgrimage was firmly established. A monastery and seven chapels were built into the rock during the medieval period, a tremendous feat considering the difficult terrain and, as Robert of Torigny said, the 'horribly remote' location.

Visitors who made the journey might have been rewarded by hearing the ringing of the sixth-century silver bell, marking maritime miracles, while pilgrims who visited between 1172 and 1173 recorded their gifts of help from Our Lady in the Book of Miracles. Others left, and indeed still leave, tokens of gratitude and signs of their healing – humble gestures that are an international language of thanksgiving and intercession.

The Church of Notre Dame opens onto the Terrace of Saint Michael, who traditionally offers protection from a high place to the north, while the interior walls of Saint Sauveur are painted with scenes relating to local stories. Today, visitors can climb the 216 steps to reach the shrine on their knees, as the early penitents did, but it is perhaps more pleasant to walk slowly and to appreciate the magnificent views while reflecting on the beauty beneath and above, while looking to the Tomb of Saint Amadour, the Church of the Black Madonna and the Miraculous Bell. Allow your perspective to change as you ascend.

above The Black Madonna has been held in veneration by generations of pilgrims and, with the Christ Child on her knee, she still welcomes those who come. Tradition tells that the figure was carved by Saint Amadour, who stayed in this place to venerate the Mother of Christ. Many feel the figure embodies something of the supernatural.

left The buildings of Rocamadour cling to the sides of the cliff above the River Alzou, in the Dark Valley in the Dordogne. During the twelfth century the uncorrupt body of Saint Amadour was discovered and sparked such an increase in pilgrim visitors that seven chapels were built to accommodate their needs. To reach the cluster of caves and chapels 216 stone steps take you on a breathtaking climb above the ravine. A wide, awe-inspiring landscape combines with the beauty of the local flora and fauna to create a place in which to contemplate the natural world and our place within it.

Megaliths of Carnac
Carnac, Brittany, France

At Carnac in Brittany more than 3,000 menhirs (standing stones) stretch for a distance of over 3 kilometres (1¾ miles) in parallel lines, up to 11 abreast, that run in a north-easterly alignment, inviting the notion that these may have been ancient walkways. Menhir is a Breton word meaning long (*hir*) and stone (*men*). These long stones can exceed 6 metres (19¾ feet) in height, some stand singly while others form dolmens (Celtic table stones).

The stones occupy four distinct sites at Carnac: Le Menec, Kermario, Kerlescan, and Petit Menec (where the mossy stones lie within a wooded glade). It is thought that the looting of stones for other purposes may have formed the gaps that isolate the clusters from each other. Dating the site has been difficult. The British archaeologist, Aubrey Burl, has suggested that they were erected around 3300 BC, while material from nearby burial chambers dates to 4700 BC. The stones are made of local granite and, in places, square or circular configurations block the avenues. In some civilizations low walls are used to block the flow of spirits, which only travel in straight lines, so perhaps these blockages were meant to harness or channel spirit energy. Magnetic fields also surround the area so it is possible that this energy was used for some purpose that is now lost to us. The rows also define sightlines focusing on midwinter and midsummer moonrises and moonsets. As Caesar noted, the Celts 'define all spaces of time, not by days, but by nights, and when they calculate the dates of births, or the beginning of months or years, they are always careful to put the night before the day'.

The name 'Carnac' may come from the god Cernowain, who was known throughout the Celtic world as the horned god of fertility. Indeed, there are stories of women rubbing their bellies against the stones to aid conception. Cernowain is also god of the underworld and the astral plane, concurring with the lunar alignments theory. These all point to the theory that the use of the stones has changed over time, with the alignments being constructed over generations. As there has been no archaeological evidence of resident populations, it is assumed that the site was for special purposes outside of the mundane routine of daily life. That is not to say that religion and rites were not observed on a daily domestic basis, rather that particular attention would have been focused in a place with special qualities.

The nineteenth-century Scottish antiquarian, James Miln, spent considerable time investigating the stones and Roman remains with the help of a local boy, Zacharie Le Rouzic, who in turn developed a fascination for the place. In the 1930s Le Rouzic replaced many of the fallen stones and candidly left his mark on them with a tiny amount of cement at the base to indicate his intervention. Miln left his finds to the town, where they can be seen in the Carnac Museum of Prehistory.

right The best time to visit the stones may be outside the tourist season but if this is impossible, then access may be easier by bike. Some sections of the rock formation are within fencing to minimize erosion by the many visitors.

left Many people find individual stones have particular powers of healing, or perhaps fertility. Some come for deeply personal or religious reasons, hoping to feel something of the earth energies, magnetism and mysteries such places inspire. Others are drawn by another force, the overall spectacle and to wonder at the energies expended by those who constructed this place.

right The lines marked out by the rows of stones draw the eye onward and clearly suggest that we are being led somewhere, visually, physically or spiritually.

below right The local people who have taken the responsibility of managing the site now have a policy of not using tractors or weedkillers but allow the space to breathe and maintain its own harmony and balance. In places, gorse is allowed to thrive at the base of stones, acting as a natural barrier to those who might climb on the relics.

Santiago de Compostela
Galicia, Spain

The route to the cathedral of Santiago crosses time and space in many ways. It has been called the 'Milky Way' because the ancient starlight spills across the heavens, pointing the way to Campus de la Stella or Campus Steliae, 'Field of Stars'. The name comes from the legend of Theodomir who, in 835, had a vision of a bright star within a cluster of smaller stars. These shone above a tomb holding the relics of Saint James and two of his followers, who had ventured abroad to bring the Gospel of Christ. A church was built upon the spot. Then, in the following century, King Alfonso of Asturias declared James to be the patron saint of Spain. The town of Santiago grew along with the fame of the monastery and cathedral, drawing astronomical numbers of pilgrims.

However, the path was trodden long before these events. To the Celts and Romans this was not only a route for trade and cultural exploration, couples wanting children thought the way would lead to fecundity and symbolic use of the scallop shell may date from this belief as it is associated with the goddess Venus. Later the scallop became the scoop used to serve sustenance to weary travellers and is now the mark of a pilgrim.

On approach from the east this low-lying, most westerly part of Spain appears to sink into the sea with the setting sun and the souls of the departed, leading to the ancient belief that here was the very end of the earth and so the cape became known as Finisterre. Legend also says that the Milky Way was formed by the dust rising from walkers' feet. Traditions wax and wane and while there have always been many reasons for making pilgrimage to Santiago, the power of the route and the cathedral steeped in prayer continues to be momentous.

right The elaborate western facade of the cathedral is imposing and elaborate in its intricate detailing. The two 76-metre (250-feet) towers hold statues of Saint James' father Zebedee on the left, and his mother Maria Salome on the right. Saint James himself is on the central tower which, although shorter, elevates his position above those of his parents.

left The master craftsmen who worked Matthew, Mark, Luke and John in stone show them holding the scrolls of their gospels. Each is considered as an individual with attention given to character, pose, the modelling of garments and so on. Master Mateo was the sculptor and architect responsible for the cathedral. He was active from 1161–1217 and this work is considered to be the pinnacle of Spanish sculpture from that period.

above The relics of Saint James are preserved in a casket of tooled silver below the high altar. The saint's feast day is 25 July and many pilgrims aim to reach the cathedral on that date to witness a giant censer swing as a pendulum full of burning incense. This not only marks the occasion, it also symbolizes the pilgrims' thanks and praise rising to heaven.

above Much has been written over time about the origin of the scallop shell as a symbol for pilgrims at this site, not least that it resembles the sun setting over the sea behind Santiago, due to the city's position at Finisterre, the end of the earth. In the cathedral the shell is used repeatedly as a decorative symbol.

left The Portico de la Gloria worked in stone stands inside the western facade, with Saint James standing on the middle pier. Built between 1168 and 1188 by the Master Mateo, the carvings would originally have been resplendent with polychromatic paintwork but the beauty of the stone is not at all impoverished by the colours' fading. The portico is signed and dated 1188.

Basilica of San Francesco d'Assisi Umbria, Italy

Lush and hospitable, the landscape of Umbria has been inhabited since Neolithic times. The Etruscans came around 450 BC and built a town around a holy spring in what we now call Assisi. Later, no doubt because of the healing waters, the Romans built a temple at the spring to venerate Minerva, goddess of arts, creativity and medicine. It may be said that her establishment here was prophetic.

Early Christians supplanted the shrine with a series of churches, then around 1181 Giovanni di Bernadone was born. Now known as Saint Francis of Assisi, his profound influence still resonates. Francis rejected his comfortable, hedonistic lifestyle, aligned himself with the poor and the sick, then set about preaching Christ's message to those he met. While his eccentric behaviour, poverty and self-imposed discomfort must have raised eyebrows, he was undoubtedly charismatic. He preached to the birds, pacified a hungry wolf, communed with the natural world and revered creation in his 'Canticle of the Sun'. During a vision he received the stigmata from an angel, concealing the five wounds of Christ for the rest of his life. It is he who must be thanked for the tradition of nativity plays. These and many more aspects of Francis' life pinpointed Assisi as a spiritual hotbed. A monastery was established, along with the Order of Poor Clares (an order of nuns). As the city flourished so did the number of commissions to architects and artists such as Cimabue, Pietro Lorenzetti, Simone Martini and Giotto.

Destructive earthquakes shook Assisi in 1997 but it is a testament to the love of the town's spiritual and creative heritage that restoration was quickly instigated. Although the renovation of accumulated art treasures may seem paradoxical when viewed in the light of Saint Francis' teaching, the inspiration and enlightenment that they have offered to generations of visitors is surely invaluable.

left The Basilica of San Francesco D'Assisi is the mother church of the monastic Franciscan Order and here we see both the Upper and Lower Basilica. After Francis' canonization to sainthood in 1228, work began establishing the church on this site, formerly known as the Hill of Hell, the place for executing criminals, but now called the Hill of Paradise.

above The nave of the Upper Basilica is adorned with frescoes, most
of which were probably painted by Giotto and his workshop. The images
are based around Saint Francis' life story, the Legenda Major or Bigger
Legend, as recorded by Saint Bonaventure. The impact of such intense
imagery can be overwhelmingly moving and plenty of time should be
given to absorbing their impact.

left 'The Devils Cast Out of Arezzo', painted by Giotto di Bondone sometime before 1300, appears in the Upper Church at Assisi. Notice how the artist has separated the church from the town, which is trapped between the crowd of devils above and their shadows below. As the residents cower inside the city walls, the arm of the monk performing exorcism bridges the gap between church and laity.

left Saint Francis is shown receiving the stigmata, the wounds of Christ in another scene from the Upper Church, by Giotto. The mountain setting and the chasm beneath the saint's feet symbolize that he was set apart from the world and on a higher plane, while the rich palette lends dramatic impact. The paintings were made on fresh, wet plaster, hence the name 'fresco'.

Mount Athos Halkidiki, Greece

The conical marble mountain of Mount Athos, or Agion Oros as it is locally known, is a space set aside purely for devotion to God, and has been for more than 1,000 years. The often snow-capped mountain reaches 2,033 metres (6,670 feet) into the sky and the peninsula it stands upon is up to 12 kilometres (7½ miles) wide and stretches 50 kilometres (31 miles) into the sparkling waters of the north Aegean sea.

According to legend, Mount Athos was formed during a fight between the gods and the Gigantes, when Zeus tossed aside a mountain that had been hurled towards him by the giant Athos. Another version of this tale says that the mountain was formed when Poseidon crushed Athos with a rock. The monks who currently inhabit this most easterly peninsula of the Halkidiki have another story about how the roots of Christianity came to reach here. The early people who lived in this place worshipped the gods of antiquity. Early in the first century AD travellers making for Cyprus sheltered from a storm here – Saint John the Evangelist was taking the Virgin Mary to see Lazarus. However, Mary sensed the place to be holy and was so moved by its beauty that she asked God to let her stay. He replied, 'Let this place be your lot, your garden and your paradise, as well as a salvation, a haven for those who seek salvation'. Then an earthquake shook the land and all that was once held sacred to the pantheon of ancient deities was shattered, including the temple to Apollo.

In due course the people who lived there were baptized and began to follow Christ. The first monks arrived during the fifth century and by the fifteenth century it is estimated that there were 20,000 monks, dedicating their life to God in what became known as Mary's Garden. Political upheaval has made the island unsettled at various times, but during the early part of the twentieth century the Monks' Republic was acknowledged as a theocratic government, allowing autonomy. There are presently around 300 monks living in 20 monasteries, hermitages and cells. The peninsula can only be reached by sea, and the jagged coastline makes access limited, but living in isolation allows individuals to serve God without the distractions of the secular world.

right This monastery seems to grow from the mountainside, its teetering stasis a metaphor for the community's relationship with the outside world. The industry and dedication of the monks is laid out in the terraced kitchen gardens, built into the enduring walls, and lived in the ordered and disciplined routine of daily life as they strive for perfection.

above The word monastery comes from the late Greek *monasterion*, to live alone, *monos* meaning 'alone' and *terion* 'a place for'. Here on Mount Athos there are many states of being alone. The place and people are isolated in many ways, although a community, and many of the monks do live in complete isolation, seeking oneness with God. Here the architecture reflects that which can come through the solitary life – order, calm and rhythm.

above This aerial view of one of the monasteries on Mount Athos gives a clear idea of the intense beauty of the place. The juxtaposition of deep sea and a verdant mountain piercing the sky offers a microcosm of creation; all that is needed is provided. The flow of water against dry land is often seen as a symbol of crossing from one realm to another; visitors to Mary's Garden describe arrival as stepping into a heaven on earth.

above Artistic skills are gifts from God and religious artists see their works as service to Him and to the world. Frescoes, mosaics and stained glass sing from the walls of the holy buildings on Mount Athos, their narration illuminating the testaments, gospels and lives of the saints. It is estimated that wall decorations here occupy approximately 100,000 square metres (328,000 square feet) with stunning icons and frescoes by the Byzantine masters onwards.

Delphi Fokís, Greece

The gods who were once worshipped at Delphi and other places of antiquity are adored no longer and so the use of these sites has changed. Yet such places are still of relevance today because they speak of people's inherent need to find the divine. They teach reverence for the natural world and have doubtlessly shaped perceptions of the sacred and helped to evolve patterns of worship. Furthermore, who is to say that there is not some residing spirit of place that can nourish the souls of modern people?

Delphi sits on the side of Mount Parnassus, above the Gulf of Corinth and in the valley of the River Plistus. The site was home to a community as early as 1500–1100 BC and held sacred to Gaia, the earth goddess; Python was her serpent daughter and guardian of this beautiful place. Legend says the god Zeus released two eagles – one from the east and one from the west – and as they soared through the blue skies, they met above Delphi, which was then declared the centre of the earth. Apollo, god of sun and son of Zeus, came from Mount Olympus to Parnassus and battled with Python who fled to Delphi for safety. However, Apollo slayed her there and claimed the ground, marking the spot with

above left The Temple of Apollo extant today belongs to the fourth century BC and sits on the site of an earlier shrine. It was here that the Pythia entered a trance state through inhaling pneuma. Ancient legend claims the dead Python as the source of the fumes, which were recorded by the philosopher Plutarch, once a priest here. Geologists have validated the presence of entrancing fumes.

above The Castalian spring within this fountain house was the place to bathe before consulting the oracle. In Greek mythology, the nymph Castalia became the spring, her waters inspiring poetic genius; it is said that the poet Byron (1788–1824) immersed himself here. The spring's use predates classical Delphi, the room being lined with marble around the sixth century BC.

an omphalos stone. *Omphalos* is the Greek word for 'navel' and an omphalos stone symbolically marks the centre of the earth.

Later, Apollo learned from Pan the secrets of prophecy and built a temple that became the seat of the oracle and a centre for divination. The oracles were young high priestesses called Pythia, who would bathe in the sacred Castalian waters and sip from the Kassotis spring. Then, in a trance, words of an unknown tongue would come from the oracles' lips. These words would be interpreted by priests and served to advise kings and politicians

with such success that Delphi became the major seat of wisdom and influence, although guidance could only be given when Apollo was thought to be present. Today, visitors can absorb the atmosphere at the remains of the Temple of Apollo, the Altar of the Chians, the Stoa of the Athenians, the Tholos and the Castalia Spring. Craftsmanship and dedication, skills and sacredness are contained in the stones that mark this site. But even before the first stone was set in place or the first god conceived of, this was clearly a place of stupendous beauty, magnitude and power.

africa & the middle east

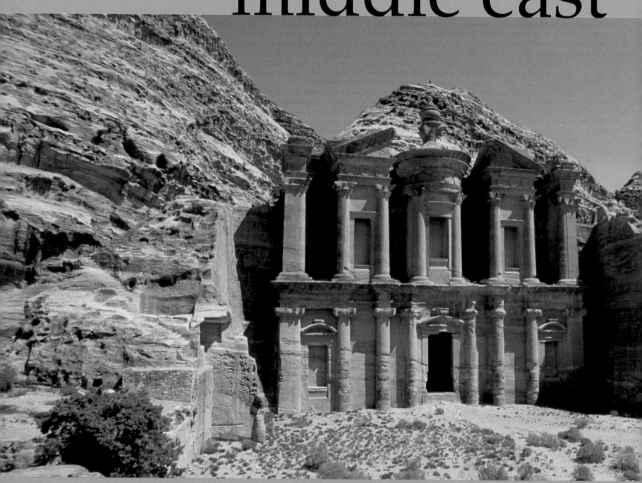

Judaism, Christianity and Islam evolved in the region known as the Middle East, which includes some of Southwest Asia, and parts of North Africa. In Africa itself, Christianity and Islam are the main faiths practised but African traditional religions still thrive too, with ancestor veneration, magic and witchcraft playing their part. The balance of those elements may be specific to particular ethnic groups as traditions vary from place to place and the sites we visit in this chapter reflect that broad spectrum.

Petra has witnessed change of devotional use over an enormous period and is thus symbolic of the places we encounter in this chapter. Human settlement in the region dates from 7,000 years BC, with Old Testament characters dwelling here. Nearby, beads of turquoise, shell and mother-of-pearl were traded; such activity may have initiated the routes that connected Petra to the outside world.

Three of these places no longer see active worship or human dwelling. At Petra in Jordan the government moved the Bedoul tribe away, during 1985, so as to excavate and restore the city, which is now a tourist destination. The town of Giza has a population of nearly five million but the ancient site is used mainly by sightseers and archaeologists. In South Africa the San People, hunter-gatherer Bushmen who first worshipped in the caves and communed with the spirit world, no longer live in the uKhahlamba-Drakensberg Park region, although their descendants and culture live on elsewhere. But this is not to say that the heart and soul have vanished from those places. For while the inhabitants of Jordan and uKhahlamba-Drakensberg Park have left no written records of cultural activity, all three of those places hold vivid accounts of their belief systems through their enduring art and architecture. Paintings, carvings and hieroglyphs speak volumes about the practice and belief of their particular faith, and spaces once filled with sacred activity can still hold an imprint of sanctity to an almost tangible degree. Our other sites in this chapter make similar use of the arts, with signs and symbols acting as easily recognizable religious markers.

In Bethlehem, minarets, domes, spires, crosses and crescents write as clearly as calligraphy across the skyline, proclaiming religious presence and affiliation, and the same can be said of Damascus. Stone Town in Zanzibar is famous for its carved doors, which show natural forms morphing into script, and the Dogon people in Mali use symbolic stylized figures across their doorways and altars. In the Old Testament of the Bible, fire is used as a symbol of God's powers, and subsequently in the New Testament it represents the Holy Spirit. The annual Festival of the Fires is still held high on the hills above Ma'alula, maintaining that symbolism, and it commemorates the flames that lit the 'route of the saints' between Jerusalem and Constantinople. Sacred geometry was the complex language taught to scholars in Timbuktu and only now are mathematicians learning how early Islamic designers formed the elaborate patterns now decipherable with twenty-first century technology. At Lalibela rock-hewn churches hide below ground level or emerge from cliff faces, and here the basic shape of the Christian cross has evolved into a range of designs expressed in paint, metal, stone and wood, their exact meaning often unknown to outsiders.

All of these uses of visual imagery are distinct in their purpose and play a different role from the narrative found, for instance, in later western art. They represent cosmic concepts and take us far beyond the earthly materials from which they are made. Just as a landscape painting may create the illusion of depth and space behind the picture plane, these signs and symbols lead us

into another dimension. While they may appear simply decorative at first glance, they are highly potent messages to those who immerse themselves and allow inner vistas to be revealed.

Early Islamic artists maintained a tradition of not depicting living creatures, including mankind, and thus sacred geometry was the visual tool that could be safely explored and exploited. The formation of those wonderful, non-repeating patterns baffled modern mathematicians and similarly their knowledge of astronomy was advanced, too. However, the Dogon people of Bandiagara Escarpment in Mali have embedded some astronomical knowledge in their culture which, according to one modern astronomer, they have no right to know about! Theoretically, they should not have been able to perceive a certain star's existence without sophisticated apparatus, but the knowledge might have been shared with cultures from around the Nile Valley. The ability of 'primitive' cultures to amaze today's scholars is a wonder in its own right, and perhaps more myths will be revealed as truths with the unfolding of time.

Ritual and ceremony are often specific to certain locations. While every place of worship has something in common with others of its denomination, some sites are unique due to a particular person or event. So, for example, in Bethlehem at the Dome of Rachel, it is thought that wearing a red thread taken from a length that has encircled the tomb will bring protection throughout pregnancy. Similarly at Lalibela those seeking fertility will bathe in a pool outside a church dedicated to the Virgin Mary. In the Islamic tradition worshippers wash before prayer and at the Omayyad Mosque in Damascus, the Ablutions Fountain stands in the courtyard for use before entering the building. Once inside, prayerful prostration and symbolic physical gestures are designed to give deeper meaning to a reverential state of mind and soul. This is by no means unusual but what is unique to this mosque is the Shrine to John the Baptist. He came from a Jewish background, baptised Jesus Christ and is recognized as a prophet by Christianity, Islam and the Baha'i tradition, and so we see a place of interfaith significance hosted by followers of Mohammed. It is encouraging to read this sign of religious tolerance and mutual respect as being symbolic of future harmony. Widely believed to have been the cradle of human evolution, Africa is the continent with the longest spiritual time span and a history of moving forwards. If we can allow ourselves to embrace, learn from and work with those outside our own faith, then we can move towards the future with optimism and confidence.

left to right Omayyad Mosque, Damascus, Syria; Ma'alula, Syria; Timbuktu, Mali; Lalibela, Semmien Wollo Zone, Ethiopia.

Petra Jordan

Half-built and half-carved, the ancient city of Petra emerges from a rocky landscape, where caves and gorges were dwellings long before records began. This is considered to be the place where the Old Testament prophet Moses struck a rock with his stick, miraculously releasing water to quench the Israelites' thirst, and it is also thought to be the resting place of his sister Miriam. The connection with Moses, such an important figure for several major faiths, continues to add an extra charge to an astonishing place. Petra was built by the Nabateans around the middle of the second century BC as a caravan city on the cusp between other trading places, as well as being a site dedicated to early deities. The Nabateans established temples, sanctuaries and burial places. When Christianity came, around the fourth century, there was inevitably a shift in devotion with churches inhabiting former tombs and temples, the old gods being superseded.

Petra is unique in its atmosphere and architecture. The local sandstone has been carved into staggering structures bearing an almost incongruous-looking Hellenistic influence. These have been buffed and eroded by time and the elements so that they now sit softly in the wider context of the landscape.

So what can today's visitors expect to find? The Siq is a unique mountain gorge, dotted with sculpted gods and niches. It narrows and darkens, setting the scene for the burst of light and drama that opens on to the columns and carvings of the Treasury, which was in fact a temple built around the first century BC. Then there is the monastery (the Al-Dayr), the amphitheatre, a marketplace, churches and tombs. Look too for the stone stairways that climb the mountain and the natural whirling patterns that flow across the walls and caves. Throughout the city you can see channels and pipes installed to continue the quenching that Moses began, as told in the Book of Exodus.

right The Siq is over 1 kilometre (⅔ mile) long, a deep dark fissure in the mountain which builds anticipation en route to the Treasury, or Kazneh. Linger here a while and seek the niches carved with gods, incised board-games and the phenomenal patterns in the stone. Then be dazzled by the glorious facade of the Treasury, which has stood in the sunshine for about 3,000 years.

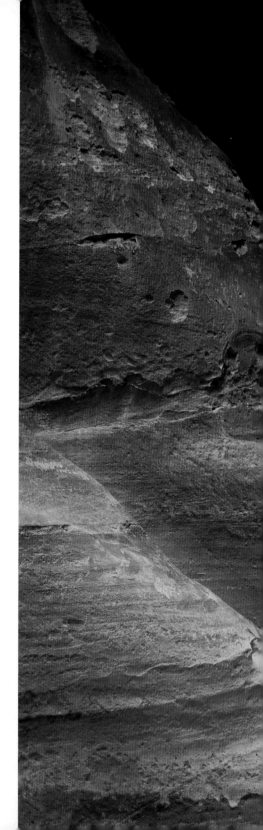

left The Al-Dayr was made as a tomb rather than a monastery, and it is thought that crosses inscribed inside may have prompted the misnomer. The masons worked down from the 45-metre (147½-feet) height where a huge urn crowns the top. Notice the counterbalance between the natural strata and the linear carving.

above Inside the tombs are niches and chambers, or loculi, venerating the dead, along with altars and carved gods. The Nabatean language derived from Aramaic, and inscriptions would have been placed in the walls but have been lost over time, perhaps moved by those who used the spaces for Christian worship, which means we cannot tell who was laid to rest here.

Bethlehem

Bethlehem Municipality,
West Bank

This town holds the tomb of the Old Testament matriarch Rachel, saw the birth of Christ and became a place of prayer for Mohammed, making Bethlehem a significant site for Judaism, Christianity, Islam and the Baha'i faith. It has borne witness to deeply powerful cosmic events that resonate throughout the world today and it still bears many physical marks of these phenomena.

The Book of Genesis tells that after Rachel's death in childbirth with her third child, she was buried on the road to Ephrath, the early name for Bethlehem, and her husband Jacob set up a memorial stone there. Still called the Tomb of Rachel, it continues to be a point of pilgrimage, especially for women praying for fertility and safe pregnancy (Rachel was childless for many years before giving birth to two sons). It is said that Rachel shed tears for the exiled Jews as they passed her tomb.

left Bethlehem's skyline serves to indicate the town's mixed faith community. Although the crescent moon had been used symbolically long before the Islamic faith came into being, it was adopted because the first sighting of the waxing crescent after a New Moon marks the first day of the month in the Islamic lunation. For Christians, the cross proclaims Christ's death and resurrection.

In the fields around Bethlehem the birth of Jesus Christ was announced by angels to astonished shepherds who ran to the town and found the child there. Later, astronomers from far afield identified a wondrous, auspicious star and followed it to the town, also in search of Jesus. The site considered to be the exact birthplace is now marked by the Church of the Nativity.

Bethlehem is the place where Mohammed rested to pray on the night that he made his journey to Jerusalem from Mecca, in the first year of the Islamic calendar. Some say that he flew on a winged steed, Buraq, or it may be that his visit was a spiritual one in which he was lifted to heaven by the Angel Gabriel. The confluence of

above The main apse of the Church of the Nativity was once highly decorated with elaborate mosaic pictures and patterns across the walls and floor. Surviving sections, such as this, are protected from visitors' tread by glass screens through which they can be viewed. The patterns incorporate sacred symbols and geometry along with natural forms.

so much that is significant to the Abrahamic faiths means that Bethlehem is not only highly charged with religious vibrancy, it is also a place that challenges the faith groups' approach to mutual tolerance, respect and adherence to God's word.

left The birth of Christ was announced to shepherds by supernatural forces in fields like this outside Bethlehem. Imagine the bewilderment of stars on a clear night being outshone by the glory of God and the singing of an army of angels! And then the further thrill of being the first to visit Christ, nestled into an animals' feeding trough.

below Over the years the Tomb of Rachel has been modified from the original stone monument set up by Jacob, and due to political unrest in the region it now needs fortification. However, an ancient tradition continues – that of encircling the tomb with a scarlet thread and then wearing a length around the neck or wrist for protection, especially during pregnancy.

Omayyad Mosque
Damascus, Syria

Damascus is the world's oldest continually occupied city and much of its story is held in microcosm within the Omayyad Mosque. Hadad, the stormy Syrian god of thunder and lightning was worshipped here in ancient times. When he was supplanted by the Roman deity, Jupiter, Hadad's sanctuary became the Temple of Jupiter. It was to Damascus that Saul was heading when he was struck by the blinding vision which led to his becoming a disciple of Christ and eventually taking the title Saint Paul. During the fourth century AD Christians used the Roman temple as a church, preaching Christ's message of love. Eventually, Muslims shared the site, both faiths entering at the same gate but worshipping respectfully apart. In time, the congregations outgrew the building and the Christians moved elsewhere, receiving a new church in compensation. The Omayyad caliph, Abdul Malek bin Marwan, refined the building to encourage worship and the surrender of self to God. Fortunately for us, many marks of history were left and so this great building eloquently recounts its past.

The approach to the mosque is via the noisy, bustling souk, but when you pass the Roman pillars the noise fades, the space opens out and the entrance to the mosque beckons you across a sunny courtyard. Once inside, your eyes are thrilled by the engaging Koranic scripts and intense geometric patterns that characterize Islamic art. However, the site is once again shared with Christians and tourists are welcome too, so the building serves the widest community.

The mosque may have had a stormy past but the fact that these disparate groups can visit here and feel welcome is a life-affirming joy. In 2001 Pope John Paul II visited the mosque and called for better mutual understanding and partnership between Christianity and Islam, for the good of the human family; the Omayyad Mosque is exemplary.

right The Omayyad Mosque sits in splendour within bustling and vibrant Damascus. More than 100 monuments indicate the area's varied sacred past, while today's worshippers continue that richness. A visit to the mosque has been described as a unifying multifaith moment, and a chance to celebrate that presence within the landscape of a multi-ethnic but unforgettably predominantly Muslim country.

above The ablutions area stands in the courtyard outside the western entrance to the haram, the holy site. Sacred geometry underpins Islamic design, from the mosaic patterns to the floor plan to the domes. Just as sounds can be made to echo around a space, sacred geometry magnifies the power of prayer and other sacred energies as the spiritual is transcribed into the physical world.

right The historic veracity of the claim that John the Baptist's head is buried here is less important than the symbolic status that the shrine bears for members of the Abrahamic faiths. John was a first-century Jewish preacher, prophet and ascetic who baptized Christ, among others. The shrine attracts those who pray communally, those who desire solitude and those who, perhaps, seek faith.

right A classical influence is seen on the Corinthian pillars, which support the elaborately decorated hexagonal Treasury building. Beyond the *sahn*, or courtyard, is the Al-Arous Minaret from which the muezzin calls a chant to bring the faithful to prayer, facing each direction in turn. The role of the muezzin is an ancient one dating back to Mohammed's own lifetime.

Ma'alula Syria

Fifty kilometres (30 miles) north of Damascus, in the Qalamoun Mountains, is a town where the inhabitants still speak the Aramaic language of the New Testament and use the caves and streets that bore witness to the rejoicing, traumas and miracles of early Christian life. There are relics of the past here, churches, shrines and so on, but what is more compelling is that many of these are still in use as living, breathing signs of an active and vital sacred realm.

The Mar Sarkis Monastery was built during the fourth century on the site of a former pagan temple, its altar kept in constant use since that time. It is irrefutably moving to feel so direct a link with the generations of worshippers who have come to that altar with their joys and sorrows, receiving sacraments according to their need. Those who feel it recognize the impact of how prayer mysteriously imprints itself upon a place.

left The Convent of Saint Tekla is situated just a little way from the mountain chasm. It is uplifting to think that Tekla's faith was strong enough to survive the persecution of the Roman soldiers and that in deep distress she was able to call upon God for a miracle. However, she was able to draw strength from her difficulties and dedicated her life to serving God.

However, the direct link with early Christianity is even older than the altar. Around the year 45 AD a young woman called Tekla, who had heard the preaching of Saint Paul, travelled to Antioch where she was persecuted by the Romans for her Christianity. A miraculous downpour quenched the flames set to burn her in the town square and she fled to her village. But the Roman soldiers persued her and Tekla was chased through the mountains. On reaching a dead end she prayed for another miracle. An almighty crack split the mountain open allowing her to reach safety.

From then on she dwelt in a cave and dispensed blessing, healing and wisdom to those who were drawn by word of these

above Ma'alula radiates from the mountainside welcoming the pilgrims who seek its sacredness. The Aramaic dialect spoken here has never been written by the locals yet is vital to biblical scholars. Tradition is kept alive here too, such as the Cross Day and the Festival of Fires set on the mountain tops to remember the route of saints between Jerusalem and Constantinople.

events. Ma'alula means 'entrance' in Aramaic and refers to the miraculous chasm. This place is both a gateway to deeper understanding and truly entrancing.

above Ma'alula is a predominantly Christian community of about 2,000 people in a mainly Muslim country and pilgrims from many faiths come here for blessings and to make offerings. The town has active monasteries; this image shows the Mar Tekla and the Mar Sarkis, the latter named after a Roman soldier who was executed for his beliefs. Many of the churches, shrines and sanctuaries have an almost timeless feel, having survived the centuries.

right The Aramaic meaning of Ma'alula is 'entrance' and this opening lends its name to the town. It is the chasm that cracked open allowing Tekla to escape persecution. At the same time a spring burst from the rock and pilgrims drink from this as it seeps into the cave where Tekla lived; her grave is a nearby place of pilgrimage too.

Giza Necropolis Cairo, Egypt

That the Giza plateau is home to some of the world's most astounding manmade structures is largely due to the River Nile. It would flow and flood these parts bringing fertility to the land, enabling transport and playing a pivotal role in ancient Egyptian cosmology. As the Nile flowed north, the sun rose on one side of the river, set on the other and passed through the underworld overnight to begin the cycle again the next day. The first appearance in the year of Serpet, the bright star we call Sirius, announced from the heavens the annual floods which brought irrigation and crop-enriching silt. This marker of time was crucial in the development of the ancient calendar around 5,000 years ago. So we see a very focused cyclical background to life's rhythms, connecting immeasurable forces of vast cosmic significance to the population and its earthly survival.

How does all of that relate to the stupendous structures that spark our admiration and imagination? The ancient Egyptians were great mathematicians, architects and scientists and they lived in a hierarchical society where royalty was second only to the deities. The artists and scribes tell us this and that death in this world meant starting life in the next. So the great rulers needed to be prepared for this transformation by being embalmed and properly equipped, with a likeness being preserved to ensure the continuation of life itself.

This is where the pyramids play their part, for not only are they burial chambers, they are focal points for the mythology and religion that venerate the gods of sun, moon and stars too. Here at Giza there is an alignment of pyramids to Khufu, Khafre and Menkaure, along with the Great Sphinx, temples and more, rising splendidly and marking time in a way unimaginable to those who built and used them. As an Arabic proverb says, 'Man fears Time, yet Time fears the Pyramids'.

left With their square bases and triangular faces the pyramids are aesthetically stable, solid and iconic. But they are not only a visual treat; they are statements of purpose, imagination and faith. The apparently simple exteriors house a wealth of art, science and magic within walls precision-built from blocks of limestone and granite under a sizzling sun.

above Of the Seven Wonders of the Ancient World, the Pyramid of Khufu has the distinction of being the only one to survive. Khufu, also known as Cheops, ruled from 2585–2566 BC. Built to launch just one man on his mystical journey to the next world, the pyramid houses a network of corridors and shafts, with the King's Chamber at its heart.

above With the head of a Pharaoh and the body of a lion, this huge creature guards a small temple between its mighty paws. Awe-inspiring and baffling, some say that its lion body is a reflection of the heavenly Leo. At 73 metres (240 feet) long and 20 metres (652 feet) high, this enormous, inscrutable beast is largely made from one great rock which sits on quarried stones.

above With a footprint of 45,000 square metres (53,820 square yards), the Pyramid of Khafre is the second largest pyramid at Giza. Unlike the others, this structure retains some of its polished limestone facing. This would have given a dazzling radiance to the sides illuminated by strong sunlight, complemented by crisp degrees of shadow. Brilliant by day, their presence must have been luminous and mystical by starlight.

Bandiagara Escarpment
Mopti region, Mali

Caves pepper the sandy Bandiagara Escarpment, a 150-kilometre (93-mile) cliff that runs through Mali and which has been occupied since prehistory. The area is home to the Dogon people, who displaced the Tellem tribes during the fourteenth century.

The caves are set aside as shrines sacred to the ancestors, the Dogon dwelling around the cliff in huts of mud and thatch. Their traditional belief system is complex and rich with a mutually sustaining relationship between the living and the dead. Their animist tradition acknowledges Amo as the god of sky, Nomo the water deity and Lewe, god of earth. The Hogon, or priest, lives outside the village and sleeps alone so that Lewe can impart wisdom overnight. Local plants and stones are inhabited by spirits associated with Lewe while sacred animals may contribute protection or divination.

Po Tolo is the name given to a tiny, dense star, which dances an elliptical path around Sirius, tilting on its axis and taking 50 years to complete its course. This cycle is celebrated with ceremonies and spinning dances by the Dogon, who have an astonishing insight into astronomy. Their lore says that news of the star was brought to them by stellar spirits connected to Nomo and that Po Tolo, made of the heaviest white metal in creation, is the seed from which the Milky Way grew. While this knowledge is in part explained by the notion that the Dogon may have come to Bandiagara from the Nile Valley, where Sirius played a pivotal role in ancient cosmography, Po Tolo, known to the scientific community as the tiny, white and dense Sirius B, is a relative newcomer to astronomers' sky charts and does follow the path described by the Dogon. Moreover, it is not visible to the naked eye and therein lies an intriguing mystery as to how the Dogon gained their intimate astronomical wisdom.

right The Dogon build their villages on rocky ground close to the escarpment to be near their ancestors and to maximize arable land. The dwellings are made of mud and thatch and many of the communal buildings serve either men or women only. Dogon culture is peaceful, mutually respectful and full of ritual designed to maintain harmony.

left Sacred imagery is worked into the doors, such as Lebe the snake and the guardian crocodile who protects those within. Dogon craftsmen are respected within the community because in retelling mythology in tangible visual language, they reinforce it and they too become woven into lore. Ripples of influence have reached the outside world, with Dogon style influencing Western art forms.

right Dogon altars hold sacred imagery. The central figure shows a stilt dancer imitating a long-legged tingetange bird at a Dama ceremony, which makes a bridge for the dead to reach the next world. The Dama is primarily to allow the dead to find peace but such occasions inevitably act as tourist attractions. The stylized geometric figures represent the first human beings.

below right Caves within the Bandiagara Escarpment act as eyes into another world and the Dogon people now reserve them as shrines for their ancestors. The area is rich in many ways as both culture and landscape are unique and visually exciting, making the area magnetic to tourists. However, some art forms hold such significance that they are hidden away from outsiders.

Timbuktu Mali

Salt was the commodity that brought camel trains to Timbuktu, gold and ivory the currency exchanged for that essential treasure. Blessed by topography, Timbuktu was an ideal place for trade by virtue of its proximity to the River Niger, thus wealth and fame brought scholars, and scholars established seats of learning, libraries, schools and mosques.

Sankore University was established in 989 AD and this was a pivotal point around which the scholars of Islam moved, with imams leading their students through the sacred texts and also teaching astronomy, logic, maths and sacred geometry. Timbuktu became a mine of spiritual nourishment and development and a fount of literature too. Many books were written and traded, and all the time the Sahara yielded yet more salt. Gold continued to make its gleaming way here; knowledge, faith, essentials, luxury and wealth shone, each with its own resonance on the spectrum of desirability.

left Djenne has been described as Timbuktu's sister city. The Great Mosque is the world's largest mudbrick building and needs constant maintenance, an act culturally embedded in an annual festival. Pits of plaster are stirred by young men playing within them and, once ready, the plaster is smeared over the face of the building by men climbing the protruding scaffold posts.

By 1330 the Mali Empire was flush with the grandeur of this success, the sacred city of Timbuktu being one of Islam's most important spiritual centres. However, over time, more than 100 libraries lost documents to European seats of learning, prompting the removal and concealment of more texts than we shall ever know, for safe keeping. Many were stashed in desert caves and underground tunnels. Today, a concerted effort is made by the Timbuktu Manuscripts Project to preserve 700, 000 Islamic manuscripts held here, some dating back to the thirteenth century, so that today's scholars and theologians can benefit from ancient knowledge.

above Djinguereber Mosque, a notable seat of learning in Timbuktu, is made almost entirely from mud, straw and wood, yet can accommodate 2,000 worshippers. The Emperor of Mali is thought to have paid 200 kilograms (441 pounds) of gold for it to be built in 1327. Like the rest of Timbuktu, it faces a threat from the encroaching desert.

While many in the outside world believe Timbuktu to be no more than a far flung myth, West African lore knows that 'Salt comes from the north, gold from the south, but the word of God and the treasures of wisdom come from Timbuktu'.

above The focal point for Islamic propagation, Sankore Mosque was
home to the early university, dating from 989 AD. As most of the traders
who passed through Timbuktu were followers of Islam, sacred buildings
flourished, so function followed need and the city's holy reputation grew
and religious scholars gravitated here. Trade in books became second only
to the salt–gold market.

above Djenne is known as Africa's Eternal City and the Great Mosque
was built on the site of a former palace which was destroyed to make room
for worship. The current edifice was constructed in the early years of the
twentieth century, over the ruins of one built 700 years earlier. Only members
of the Muslim faith are allowed into the building.

Lalibela Semien Wollo Zone, Ethiopia

Originally called Roha but renamed for King Lalibela (1181–1221) who instigated the making of these unique rock-hewn churches, this place continues to be an active holy site of pilgrimage and devotion. Following the rise of Islam in Jerusalem, King Lalibela intended that his home town would become 'New Jerusalem'. So from the volcanic rock that forms the Ethiopian highlands were gouged 12 unique and wonderful churches, tunnels, catacombs and hermitages. Many of the churches are subterranean, their makers splitting and carving the rock with skilful knowledge lost to today's builders. Each church has its own remarkable features. How exactly did Lalibela come to have such a powerful vision and how was he able to motivate others into such an extraordinary project in this hard and harsh environment?

Shortly after birth, Lalibela's mother found him surrounded by bees. Aware of old beliefs, she interpreted this as a sign of the child's future greatness so he was marked as significant from an early age, his name meaning 'the bee recognizes his sovereignty'. His brother, the king, feared that this charismatic boy threatened his position on the throne and tried to kill Lalibela, eventually resorting to poison. During the ensuing three-day coma, Lalibela was lifted to heaven where God instructed him to establish the unique churches and told him how to design, build and decorate them. On awaking, his conviction and zeal were so infectious to those around him that the vision became reality. Tradition says that the project moved swiftly as angels continued the work overnight, while the labourers rested. Whatever the truth behind the stories, Lalibela's mission continues. Pilgrims swarm to this holy site from far and wide, including the Ethiopian Orthodox Tewahedo Church, which has a membership of over 40 million people. Clearly, the man and the place are powerfully gifted to exert such far-reaching attraction.

right Unlike so many places of worship that proudly pierce the skyline, some of Lalibela's churches are tucked away underground as if within the very core of creation. While its makers may have kept their heads down for fear of Christianity's enemies, their inventiveness and determination is an ongoing affirmation of faith. This cruciform roof indicates the cardinal points while daily rhythms flow around it.

above It is said that Abba Libanos Church was built in a single night by angels helping Lalibela's wife, Maskal Kebra, Abba Libanos being one of the most highly venerated Ethiopian saints. Visitors may see the mysterious light that seems to burn through its own power, and elsewhere various crosses which have evolved into a mystical language each holding its own meaning.

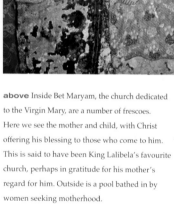

above Inside Bet Maryam, the church dedicated to the Virgin Mary, are a number of frescoes. Here we see the mother and child, with Christ offering his blessing to those who come to him. This is said to have been King Lalibela's favourite church, perhaps in gratitude for his mother's regard for him. Outside is a pool bathed in by women seeking motherhood.

above Standing at ground level, notice how this church is still attached at the top to the mountain, whereas the sides have been cut cleanly away, lending dignity and presence. Some say that the churches were made by local people, others say it was the Knights Templar or stonemasons from as far away as India. Tradition says that heavenly angels shared the workload.

Stone Town Zanzibar, Tanzania

In the Indian Ocean lies the archipelago of Zanzibar, where Pemba and Zanzibar itself are the largest islands. Zanzibari culture is a marriage of religion with influence from Africa, Asia and Europe, fed by centuries of bustling seaborne trade. Cloves, nutmeg and cinnamon are among the exquisite exotic exports, although in the past, this was a place for slave trade too. As such, Zanzibar bears the scars of iniquity and suffering. However, as it served as a base for the antislavery campaign it is somewhat symbolic of the abolition of that shameful activity.

Today, Stone Town is the cultural core of the island of Zanzibar and predominantly an Islamic community where the historic fusion of cultures has eroded divisions to the point where minority faiths, such as Christianity and Hinduism are gently accepted. The town itself is enjoyed by tourists for its unique status as a fascinating historic town, while further afield wonderful beaches and exotic wildlife bring the sacred gifts of the natural world into sharp focus.

This is a place where living faith has been allowed to shape commercial practice in an increasingly secular world. Misali is a small island in the archipelago where coral reefs are home to rich fish stocks and other exotic treasures. However the use of dynamite guns by fishermen was found to be destroying the ecosystems and depleting stocks. In the light of failed government intervention, religious leaders looked to the Koran for guidance on the matter, preaching that if God's gifts are to be treated with due respect, then harvesting the seas should be sustainable and must honour creation. This beautiful notion and the resulting change in practice has improved harvests and sealife has become enriched, generating tourism and, therefore, valuable income. Moreover, the community enjoys the benefits of fusing sacred duties with sustainable commerce.

left The waters around Zanzibar are home to a host of exotic turtles, fish and coral ecosystems. In recent years the tranquility and balance has been shattered by the use of dynamite in fishing, which has been reducing biodiversity. However, Koranic wisdom has now guided the Islamic community back to sustainable fishing methods, yielding increased stocks and restoring natural harmony.

above Opened on Armistice Day, Stone Town Peace Memorial Museum was built to commemorate the First World War. It gives an overview of Zanzibar's history and covers slavery, the cultivation of spices, traditional crafts, key cultural buildings and the sultans, missionaries and explorers who have had an influence on the the life of Zanzibar's people.

above The labyrinthine passages of Stone Town lead to mosques, bazaars and bustle, the business of which seems to be encapsulated in traditional carving. Over 500 exquisite doors can be found and while the level of craftsmanship may once have been a status statement, we can trace the patterns' roots in the natural world and enjoy the joyful flow into text.

above The Kizimkazi Mosque is thought to be the oldest Islamic building on the coast of East Africa. Here we see the trefoil mihrab, the niche indicating the direction for prayer, which bears an inscription dated 1107. Designed to symbolize the gateway to Mecca, the form of this particular mihrab was influential on many of Stone Town's mosques.

below These painters could depict with sophisticated accuracy, therefore we must assume that distortions such as elongated bodies had a purpose. A common thread connecting all artists is the desire to communicate and to influence some aspect of life. If images such as this represent portals to another reality, they invite visitors to take a leap of faith and link with other cultures.

uKhahlamba-Drakensberg Park
kwaZulu-natal, South Africa

uKhahlamba means 'barrier of spears' in isiZulu tongue and the name refers to the soaring spiked profile of the mountain range that forms the border between Lesotho and South Africa. It is referred to as Drakensberg or 'Dragons Mountain' by the Afrikaans. For generations of San people, this was home for over 4,000 years. Grasslands sprawl at sky level, water leaps down chasms into river valleys and each element teems with life.

The San people recognized the value of this vitality. It sustained their physical existence and contained the secrets of the spiritual world. We know this from what they have left us. The caves and rock shelters used by the San contain a huge concentration of

paintings. While they can be enjoyed on a purely aesthetic level, they are best read with some knowledge of the culture of the aboriginal people who made them. The San understanding of cosmology works on three planes, that of everyday existence plus one above and one below. When a sacred beast was killed a link between realms was opened up and the shaman could act as intermediary between the spiritual and material worlds. The eland was thought to be the closest animal to God and its flesh, skin and fat were sacred spiritual currency, used in rites of passage, initiation and possibly the binding of pigment into paint. At first glance a painting may appear to show a hunting

scene, but look closer and see shamans flying or falling alongside patterns and symbols now widely recognized as characterizing trance and hallucination. Human figures blend with animal forms, men leap and spatial norms give way to layering so that time and space are compressed, verisimilitude giving way to another reality.

left The vital energy that the San artists aspired towards in their art was found in greatest concentrations in the eland, and the shaman needed to harness that in order to enter the spirit world. Tests have shown that blood was sometimes used as pigment. Depicting a creature with its own ichor would have flooded an inherently powerful image with extra potency.

above The exceptional natural beauty of the uKhahlamba-Drakensberg Park is a rich, varied and dramatic haven for wildlife, much of which is threatened elsewhere in the world. The Barrier of Spears mountain range, which is 1,000 kilometres (621 miles) long and up to 3,482 metres (11,424 feet) high, houses an astonishing wealth of rock paintings which tell of the beliefs of aboriginal San people.

asia

The immense and awe-inspiring gifts of creation have fed the minds and souls of the Asian people, and this is reflected in the way their sacred lands are marked. Over 3,500 years ago, Hinduism began in Northern India and spread as far southeast as Indonesia, with various traditions being established along the way. Buddhism evolved from the Hindu faith in the late sixth and early fifth centuries BC and extended to Burma, Cambodia and Indonesia, then on to China, Korea and Japan, coexisting with indigenous traditions such as Daoism, Confucianism and Shintoism. The landscapes of these places are now honoured with temples, pagodas, stupas and shrines, according to the different faiths that put down roots and reached up to the heavens.

The River Ganges, India's sacred channel, is the physical manifestation of the goddess Ganga, daughter of the Hindu mountain god Himalaya. The waters run 2,507 km (1,558 miles) from the Himalayas to the Bay of Bengal, the sacred rivers Yamuna and Brahma Putra contributing along the way. For centuries, it has been a setting for ritual cleansing, rites of passage and devotion.

In such a huge and populous continent as Asia

it is unsurprising to come across a wide variety of conceptions of the sacred. This diversity is reflected in the way that sacred spaces are marked and used. All of the major faith groups have had at least a foothold in these lands; while many can trace their traditions to an historical figure, others know their beliefs to have been practised from the beginning of time. Those with their origins in India, China and Japan – including Zoroastrianism, Hinduism, Jainism, Buddhism, Sikhism, Taoism and Shinto – see the divine contained in all creation. The Abrahamic faiths, Islam, Judaism and Christianity, forbid idolatry and so, broadly speaking, have struggled with the notion of an object or place being inherently sacred.

Historically, conduits such as the trade routes opened up opportunities for the movement of ideas, and mendicant monks ventured with sacred texts to far-flung places. Asia reveals a wealth of lusciously and luxuriously decorated devotional buildings, from the elaborate designs used by Islamic architects to the sensuous carvings in Jain, Sikh and Hindu temples, the cosmic architecture of Buddhism and the colourful symbolism of Shinto Torii and Taoist shrines. Voyaging first to Uzbekistan, we meet the wonders of dazzlingly intricate sacred geometry. This goes beyond pattern for pleasure, serving a far deeper purpose. Islam strives for oneness with Allah and while proscribing

idolatry, acknowledges the power of the visual world and its ability to touch our souls. And in recognition of mankind's instinct to withdraw to a special space for worship, creative scholars aimed to express the essence and infinity of Allah's greatness in nonrepeating pattern. It is important to understand that the power of sacred geometry does not stop at surface decoration but is a multidimensional concept designed to enhance the spiritual power of the building. Domes, for instance, can act as sound reflectors, returning vibration to the centre. The same principles are applied to the floorplan and proportion of all aspects of the architecture, inviting our minds to connect with the structures that form the tissues, cells and atoms of creation, and thus with the creator. We can only wonder about the extent of sacred geometry once used in the remote Afghan valley around the Minaret of Jam. Time and troubles have shaken most of the former city to the ground but archaeologists have picked up traces of other faith groups' sacred signs and hope to clarify the story of this fascinating place.

The artists who decorated the Jain, Hindu, Sikh and Buddhist temples were never inhibited in the use of human and godly forms. The figures covering the surfaces of these buildings may be playful, mystical, erotic or narrative. They blend the natural and supernatural worlds, affirming the presence of the divine in all matter; the artist coaxes that presence into visible form.

The sacred River Ganges makes its way from the Himalayas to the Bay of Bengal and along its route are sites for bathing, festival, pilgrimage and launching the dead to another shore. The Hindu texts, the Vedas, stress the divinity of creation and the fact that its marvels exceed our comprehension. They also tell of the waters of the earth being created before all else, and of how everything depends upon water. In the Sikh tradition Guru Nanak compares the soul's thirst for God to a fish's need for water while Buddhists use water as a symbol of consecration and sharing. All religions recognize water as being not only vital to life but also our spiritual health. As we acknowledge the thirst experienced around the world we become charged with our share in the responsibility for remedial action. Many international and local organizations are now supporting faith groups in asserting the right to manage resources according to their religious tradition. That pilgrimage and ritual around sacred waters continue, despite the difficulties, can be seen as an increased affirmation of faith in life's cycles.

The mythology we hear of at Ha Long Bay in Vietnam depends on its watery location, and there seem to be as many stories as there are islands, caves and life forms along this uniquely beautiful stretch of coastline. Also hallowed for its natural features is the the sacred Mountain Sri Pada in Sri Lanka. It symbolizes the evolution of belief from age to age and, perhaps more importantly, the sharing of sacred space by many faiths. This is something we see in temples from Nepal to East Asia, where a gentle syncretism softens the margins between faiths so that, over the years, sites have seen subtle shifts in practice, devotion and ritual. For instance, Borobodur in Java, which was rooted in Hinduism, is now a Buddhist destination. Designed along cosmographic principles it invites pilgrims to climb a symbolic mountain temple beneath the open sky. Also in the open are the mountains in China and Japan where worship began before records. Tao means the 'way of nature', and the 1995 Taoist Statement on Ecology declares that Taoism judges affluence by the number of species. In Taoist temples of the Wudang Mountains of China, and also at Fuji-San and the Kii Mountains of Japan, we come across monastic complexes and shrines where the powers of nature are recognized, harnessed and magnified through living in harmony with natural cycles, sustainably taking only what is needed. Rocks, water and plant life are particularly potent. So again we see the natural elements charged with symbolic powers. Perhaps the greatest lesson that we can learn from the wisdom of these sacred traditions is also the simplest; that we can honour creation by nurturing a kinship with nature.

left to right Jain Temple, Ranakpur, India; Ayutthaya, Ayutthaya Province, Thailand; Ha Long, Bay of the Descending Dragon, Vietnam; Borobudur, Java.

Bukhara
Bukhara Province, Uzbekistan

Beneath the medieval city visible today sit ancient remains left by the people who occupied this land as early as the third century BC, and those traces tell of the distant cultures in which the people had their roots. In early times Bukhara was the centre of worship of Anahita, a water deity associated with fertility, wisdom and healing. Once during each lunation, her followers would discard their idols and buy new ones, in a temple rite that gave rise to commercial practice, assisted by the city standing on a trade route.

Being on the Silk Road, the ebb and flow of visiting traders and travellers from China, Iran and India brought an inevitable degree of outside influence, and there are signs of Zoroastrian, Buddhist, Manichean and Christian worship here. The city's name may be derived from *vihara*, a Buddhist monastery, or from *bukhar*, which was a fount of knowledge to Zoroastrians. Or perhaps the name comes from Baha-ud-Din Naqshband Bukhari, the fourteenth-century mystic who certainly lends his name to Naqshbandi Sufism. Apart from the fact that he spent most of his life in Bukhara, we know little of this great scholar and venerated holy man; he forbade his followers to record his life as to do so would detract them from spiritual matters. The city saw the development of other spiritual treasures too. Masters of calligraphy, poetry and miniature painting (which takes its name from minium or red lead) used their skills to express their faith and encourage faith in others, a sacred use of God-given gifts. From this richly creative cultural melting-pot a city evolved that tourists now enjoy for its piquant mix of elaborate Islamic buildings, shady pools and ancient trees, colourful bazaars and festivals of spices and silks.

left The Kaylan (or Kalon) Mosque was completed in around 1515. It is crowned with a glazed turquoise cupola that sings against the sky and the intricate geometry and calligraphy of the faience tiles. Although the city has multifaith traditions, it is known in the Islamic world as 'the noble and glorious stronghold of faith'; such architecture loudly proclaims that belief.

above Minarets developed from the tradition of the muezzin calling the congregation to prayer, as bells are rung from towers in other traditions. The height, along with the elegantly decorated shapes, allow these structures to transcend their material roots and become conductors between heaven and earth, as though their energies cannot be contained but must be vocalized.

left Khalif Niazkul built the Chor Minor Madrasah in 1807, and this entrance also lead to a mosque and a sacred garden. A madrasah is a school, and at one time there were about 60 in Bukhara. Subjects studied included theology, the philosophy of law, logic, poetry and music, making the city an oasis of wisdom as well as of water.

right The Samanid Mausoleum was built between 892 and 943 for Ismail Samani, founder of the Samanid Dynasty. Its construction and design are a mix of early local tradition and Islamic innovation. The building bears a basket weave appearance, though it is made of local clay fired into wonderfully enduring brick. It stands on ancient sacred soil, the site of an earlier burial ground.

Samarkand Uzbekistan

'Region of War' is the translation of Samara Khanda, the Sanskrit name for Samarkand, one of the world's oldest cities. Dating back over 2,500 years, the city repeatedly endured attack from leaders such as Alexander the Great and Ghengis Khan but renaissance always followed its destruction. Samarkand enjoyed an advantageous location on the Asian Silk Road, connecting China with the West. One Chinese visitor, the Buddhist pilgrim Hsuan-tsang, recorded an insight into seventh-century Samarkand, describing it as a place of great treasures from distant lands, powerful horses and skilled artisans.

The scientists, artists, architects and other creative professionals were helped by the Islamic world's first paper mill being founded in Samarkand during 751, after two Chinese prisoners yielded the secrets of paper-making. This of course had great significance for the dissemination and accumulation of knowledge and sacred texts; the know-how spread from here to the rest of the Islam. During the fourteenth and fifteenth centuries the city prospered under Amir Timur (Tamerlane) who made Samarkand the capital of his expanding empire. To mark the empire's glory he imported sculptors, masons, mosaic artists, glass-blowers and ceramicists from far and wide. Under his command many sacred buildings were built and gardens laid. In fact, this city was an important point of exchange for ideas about garden design, between Persia and India.

Temur's grandson, Ulugh Beg, established a huge astronomical observatory, and his findings were of great sacred significance to members of his faith. The Koran stresses the importance of the relationship between heaven and earth, with heavenly cycles being used to calculate the Islamic calendar and the times for prayer and fasting. Ulugh Beg recorded more than 1,000 stars and charted their positions, no doubt on paper made within the city. The remains of his observatory still stand, as do his discoveries.

left At the Registan three schools, called madrasahs, stand around a square built to educate young men. The students stooped to enter the low doors to the cells as a reminder that 'Islam' means 'obedience'. A wide range of subjects were studied, including maths, astronomy, jurisprudence and theology, with the Koran being at the heart of it all. The square was also a place for public festivals and bazaars.

above Ulugh Beg built one of the earliest astronomical observatories. This image shows the underground section of the great marble sextant. Originally, the observatory was a three-storey building and a hive of activity for the scientists Ulugh Beg brought to work here, before he was assassinated in 1449. His groundbreaking research is still honoured by the lunar crater that bears his name.

above The Gur-e Amir Mausoleum boasts a fluted dome 15 metres (49¼ feet) across, encircled by inscriptions and pattern. The name means 'Tomb of the King' and it is the resting place of Timur, his sons and grandson, Ulugh Beg, the astronomer-king. Ulugh Beg placed a huge block of jade – the stone of crystallized moonlight, royalty and protection – over Timur's grave as a mark of respect.

right The majestic Bibi-Khanym Mosque is one of the world's largest and its beauty inspired comparison to the Milky Way. But overambitious design and earthquakes led to instability, so much restoration has been needed since construction in 1399–1404. The calligraphy gives way to pattern towards the top of this cupola, giving the impression of prayer floating up to heaven.

below Being complimentary to the warm hues of the tiles, the turquoise inscription is clarified by virtue of its colour. The exquisite script and lattice-work on the minaret have survived for 900 years, indicating the makers' sophisticated knowledge of materials and a long-term commitment to their faith. Local villagers have found ancient artifacts belonging to diverse faiths, but most have been sold.

Minaret of Jam Afghanistan

Afghanistan has long been cherished as the source of lapiz lazuli, the bright blue metamorphic rock that yields the entrancingly mysterious blue pigment known as ultramarine. It is the colour used by artists to depict heaven and the robes of heavenly beings, such as the Virgin Mary, in Western Christian art.

Standing at the confluence of the Hari Rud and Jam Rud rivers, the minaret soars 63 metres (206¾ feet) and has its origins in the twelfth century. It is thought that this was the location of the Sunni Muslim Ghurid dynasty's summer residence, Firzkuh, within the great Afghan capital, Turquoise Mountain, which was destroyed during the thirteenth century.

The minaret would not have originally stood in isolation but was attached to the Friday Mosque, most of which was washed away during flash floods. There is indeed evidence of further buildings here and they lie beneath layers of river sediment.

This degree of decoration epitomizes the height of artistic tradition within the region and its fine craftsmanship is brought into sharp focus by contrast with the rugged, bleak, barren mountains. The telescopic profile of the tower is gracefully decorated with repeated filigree patterns and topped with a lantern – the etymology of minaret derives from the Arabic word for 'lamp'. Koranic inscriptions picked out in stucco and

above Archaeologists continue to explore the site and the structure has been stabilized. Standing along the twelfth-century Silk Road, the minaret would have been seen by thousands of people from distant lands. Archaeological finds indicate that people from Jewish, Zoroastrian, Hindu and Buddhist traditions came here, despite the difficult terrain and climate.

embellished with ceramic turquoise quote from the Surat Maryam, which speaks of the Virgin Mary.

Jain Temple Ranakpur, India

The Jain Temple at Ranakpur is in a quiet valley between Jodhpur and Udaipur, in western India. Built around the fourteenth to mid-fifteenth centuries, it is quietly, breathtakingly beautiful. The exceptional architecture and carvings create a numinous atmosphere through the use of light filtering through white marble, creating subtle shifts in colour and shade. The saturation of design in both the interior and exterior of the building offers an intense visual experience. Each carving is unique – musicians, dancers and organic forms intricately entwine in an entrancing pattern.

The footprint of the temple covers an area approximately 60 by 62 metres (197 by 203½ feet) and from this rises a forest of 1,444 marble pillars supporting cupolas, turrets and domes. Built in honour of the Tirthankaras' conquest of the four cardinal points, the building welcomes visitors from all sides.

Tirthankaras are spiritual beings who ford the waters between this world and the realm of spiritual perfection. Dharna Shah was prompted to ask the ruler Rana Kumbha for permission to build on the land after a celestial vehicle of heavenly beings visited him in a dream. The king agreed on condition that his name should be connected to the place, hence Ranakpur. So architects and craftsmen planned, carved, lifted and polished for 50 years to bring the temple into being before its consecration to Adinath.

Adinath, the first Tirthankara, is symbolized as a bull and it was he who taught Jainism to mankind. Jainism is an ancient philosophy-religion possibly dating from the sixth century BC, which teaches that the purpose of this life is to shed physical form and allow the soul to have freedom. It teaches Ahimsa, non-violence of thought or deed towards all living things. Contemplate the gentleness of that as you visit this wonderful place.

left Each of the 1,444 columns in the Adinath Temple complex is unique and they punctuate the spaces with shimmering light that changes from warm to cool as the day progresses. Notice too how the Jain's robes lend their colour to the softly lustrous marble. This seems to reflect the idea that everything is interconnected and striving for harmony.

below The Jain Temple is a lavish and sumptuous creation that sits softly in the landscape. Still very much alive as a place of worship, visitors are asked to remove their shoes and leave leather items outside to respect the Jain's strict aversion to violence towards any living thing. Nearby is the Sun Temple, designed as a chariot carrying the god across heaven.

above and left It has been said that the beauty of this building is beyond description. While the sequence of shrines, halls and stories invites movement through the temple, the minutely detailed carvings require you to pause, contemplate and move slowly. This is not a conflict of ideas, more a reminder that fraction and whole are entirely interdependent.

right An inscription quotes the architect Depaka as saying that he wanted to build a majestic temple here. More than that, he was inspired with an astounding aesthetic genius. He created a visual unity in such a way that it flows over and through the functional space, allowing the intricacies of detailed design to mesh as a coherent whole.

The River Ganges
Northern States, India

This great river personifies and takes its name from the goddess Ganga, who was born out of the creator god Brahma's *kamandula*, or water-pot. Shiva caught her in his hair, from which she trickled to earth as Hinduism's most sacred river. High in the Himalayas, melt water runs from a cave beneath the Gangotri glacier and makes it way through the planes of northern India on a 2, 506-kilometre (1,557-mile) journey to Bangladesh and the Bay of Bengal. But before it reaches the ocean this sacred river performs endless miracles for over 350 million people. Not only does the river irrigate, drain and convey, it also heals and cleanses the living and the dead. At auspicious times, bathing in the waters can cleanse the souls of the living from sin, while the bereaved immerse the ashes of their departed for forgiveness and transport to heaven. To sip the holy water at the time of dying will assure spiritual purity, as will dying on the riverbank.

Certain points along the route hold greater potency and these are the places of pilgrimage and festival. For example, at Prayag, the holy river Yamuna joins the Ganges along with the invisible river Sarasvati. This is thought to be the site of Brahma's first sacrifice, made to celebrate creating the world. It is not surprising that this is one of the cyclical sites for celebrating the Kumbh Mela festival, the others being Haridwar, Ujjain and Nashik — all of which were sprinkled with drops of amrit, the nectar of immortality. Hindus aim to make pilgrimage and bathe in the Ganges at least once in their life. For those who are too frail to travel, the river is taken to them in a *kamandula*.

above Of the major festivals that are celebrated at Haridwar, Kumbh Mela comes once every 12 years and is the world's largest gathering. It is said that Vishnu, the Hindu preserver of the universe, graced the gods here with *darshan*, the look of a holy man or woman that bestows great blessing. People travel from afar in the hope of receiving that gift.

above *Ganga Ma* means Mother Ganges, for the river brings life. The Ganges is also the physical point at which life travels hand in hand with death and transcendence. Lanterns are lit in respectful vigil for the departed. At night the river takes on a new atmosphere and many Hindu festivals are timed to mark lunar phases.

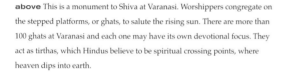

above This is a monument to Shiva at Varanasi. Worshippers congregate on the stepped platforms, or ghats, to salute the rising sun. There are more than 100 ghats at Varanasi and each one may have its own devotional focus. They act as tirthas, which Hindus believe to be spiritual crossing points, where heaven dips into earth.

above Established by Shiva, the ancient city of Varanasi – also known as Banaras and the Eternal City – sits on the banks of the Ganges and is thought to have been inhabited for anything between 3,000 and 5,000 years. This is a powerful place of pilgrimage and of festivals, marked by ritual bathing, music, fire and incense.

The Golden Temple Amritsar, Punjab, India

In Punjab in north-west India lies Amritsar, which means 'Pool of the Nectar of Immortality' and this is home to the Harimandir Sahib, the Golden Temple. The site's evolution springs from a sacred pool that was used as a focus for meditation by early ascetics, priests and philosophers including the Buddha. Much later, Guru Nanak (1469–1539) lived here and drew strength from the site's gentle but insistent powers. Guru Nanak believed in equality for all people regardless of caste, gender, religion or any other difference, and from that notion, Sikhism was born. So the essence of this sacred site crystallized and took the form of a shrine visited by disciples, despite Nanak's belief that devotion should be within oneself and not rooted to either location or ritual.

Over time the waters were contained within a lake and the temple complex grew around, and into it; the Golden Temple itself sits on a platform over the water. There is a fusion of ideas here from the Hindu and Islamic worlds, both within the architecture and the scriptures. Daily ritual includes sacred music and chanting from the holy texts, the Guru Granth Sahib, to sustain the spiritual life of worshippers. The body is sustained with hospitality for everyone who comes, and doors are situated on all four sides of the building to draw people from all quarters throughout the day until after sunset.

Around 40,000 visitors are fed each day out of temple funds and there is a free hostel too. The temple complex hums with colour, song and sharing, generating a bustling harmony. This is a place of intense spiritual excitement for Sikhs and indeed anyone who visits from around the world. The lake is still fed by the sacred spring and as it pools, reflection magnifies its powers.

above Candles are lit by the sacred waters that surround the Golden Temple to celebrate Guru Nanak's birth. Devotees walk clockwise around the building before entering to hear readings from the Guru Granth Sahib, which includes devotional poems and hymns. Written by the Ten Gurus of Sikhism and embracing Islamic and Hindu writing, the book is noted for its inclusiveness.

right The exquisite beauty of the temple complex conjures a numinous atmosphere, as gold shimmers on sacred water. The influence of Islamic and Hindu art is evident within the design and layout. Geometric pattern refers to the teleological notion of the Creator's design and purpose in the ordering of the universe down to the smallest detail.

left The foundation stone of the temple was laid in 1588 by the Sufi saint, Mian Mir, at the invitation of Guru Arjan, an event celebrated with ebullient worship and the distribution of sweets. This laid the metaphorical foundation stone for the community's continuing generous welcome, and as these pilgrims cross the Pool of the Nectar of Immortality they enter that tradition of interfaith communion.

right All who visit
the Golden Temple
are invited to share a
meal before they leave,
which is prepared
by volunteers and
provided by temple
funds. This ministry
of hospitality is a rich
and wonderful part of
the welcome extended
to all who come here,
regardless of status,
race or religion. The
kitchen is always open.

Sri Pada
Ratnapura, Sabaramauwa Province, Sri Lanka

This great teardrop-shaped mountain, also known as Adam's Peak, rises 2,243 metres (7,359 feet) out of the jungle. Its size and shape make it a stunning natural feature of the landscape. Thick with spice trees and gem mines it holds supernatural treasure too.

The indigenous Sri Lankan people, the Veddas, can claim direct descent from the aboriginal community, way back into the Neolithic period, and for them the mountain is the home of one of the island's guardian spirits. When Hinduism arrived here it was thought that this was the place at which Shiva brought the world into being through his creation dance, leaving his giant footprint in a slab of stone. Others claim that the mark was left by Buddha and that the genuine footprint is pressed into a sapphire beneath the stone that pilgrims venerate today. An Abrahamic tradition says it is the print of Adam, left after he was made to stand on one leg by God, as further punishment after expulsion from the Garden of Eden. This was where he first stepped to earth from heaven. Some Christians believe it was made by Saint Thomas when he brought Christianity here. This is a sacred site that is peacefully shared by an interfaith community.

Just as each group tells its own legends about the mountain, they also have differing names for it. Samanalakanda is 'abode of the god saman' but might equally refer to the fact that at times the air is full of migrating samanalay, or butterflies. Sri Pada means sacred footprint, while Ratnapura and Ratnagiri both refer to the vast amount of gemstones found here. Whatever it is called, the true value of any sacred site is what it means to the people who use it. During the visitors' season on an average weekend about 20,000 people climb the thousands of steps. How many footprints do they leave?

left Adam's Peak is such a feature that it has been used since early times as a landmark by passing trade ships seeking spices, ivory and gems. Today the peak draws pilgrims paying homage to whoever they claim made the huge mysterious footprint pressed into the peak. The richness of the flora and fauna add to the numinous aura of a sacred garden.

far left Many people visit annually and climb the incredibly steep 5,200 steps to the top of the peak. The climb takes several hours and the descent almost as long. Also known as Butterfly Mountain because of the number of butterflies found here, it seems appropriate that this heavenward climb should take one of its names from aerial creatures.

left Erected by Japanese Buddhists, the Cetiya stands at the base of the mountain, generating peace to climbers, and through them to the rest of the world. It offers a calm sanctuary before the exhausting, exhilarating ascent. Because bad weather brings dangerous conditions, the climb can only be made between December and May, and the season runs between the full moons.

above The full moon is honoured with a public holiday in Sri Lanka, called Poya Day. Climbing the mountain by night allows pilgrims to ascend towards the stars then greet the glorious sunrise from the peak with chanting and celebration. Opposite the sun, the mountain slides its triangular shadow in a spectacular display across the world below.

Kathmandu Valley
Nepal

Landlocked between India and the Tibetan plateau, Nepal enjoys a varied landscape and the Kathmandu Valley spreads itself over 350 square kilometres (135 square miles), 1,350 metres (4,429 feet) above sea level. The Swayambhu Purana, a Buddhist scripture, details the origin of the valley, stating that there was once a lake here, which was drained by the enlightened being Manjusri. He created a gorge in the mountain, allowing the water to escape and thus the land became habitable. The cultural mix in the valley is rich due to its being at the crossroads of ancient civilizations and there is a gentle syncretism between Hinduism and Buddhism. It has been said that there is always a festival being celebrated here, marking religious, mythical or seasonal occasions in time-honoured fashion.

However time and treatment have dishonoured the Bagnati river. This sacred water flows from its source in Bagdwar and, it is said, from the laughter of Lord Shiva, eventually joining the Ganges. It used to surge as a sacred artery bubbling with life-giving, blessing-bringing, soul-cleansing water, in which people bathed and sent their departed off to heaven. Yet in recent years it has become depleted and polluted to the point that it now seems parched of all holiness. There are projects in place to restore cleanliness and volume and it is a testament to people's faith that such steps have been taken.

In the meantime, the area's other pilgrim sites are bursting with colour and vibrant worship. Many of the temples, chaityas and stupas were built by the Newars, Nepal's indigenous people. These highly-skilled craftsmen have contributed greatly to the richness of architecture, carving and metalcraft. Through their art, music and dance they generate celebratory worship with colourful prayer flags, costume and life-affirming energy.

left Famous for its spectacular sunrises over the Himalayas, the village of Nagarkot offers a superb view of the Kathmandu Valley. Previously known as Mahamandap, it was from here that Manjusri viewed the sacred lake that he drained to create Manjupatan, the Kathmandu Valley. The verdant, fertile land is ideal for growing crops and here we see them set out on rippling terraces.

above The Bodnath, or Bouddhanath, is one of Kathmandu's most revered and ancient stupas. Stupas are funerary mounds and this one, containing the relics of a sage revered by both Hindus and Buddhists, is laid out in the sacred geometry of a mandala. Towards the top, the eyes of Buddha symbolize awareness. There are many other stupas, temples and royal palaces in the city.

above Prayer wheels at the Swayambhuath stupa in Kathmandu hold the words of a prayer or mantra, and hand-held prayer wheels may be used in dance. Turning the wheel releases the prayer, a similar act to the fluttering of prayer flags, whose symbolic colours and words are released with meaning to the gods. Traditionally, prayer flags generate peace, compassion and wisdom.

above Steps from the Pashupatinath Temple
lead down to the sacred river Bagmati. Built
during the fifth or sixth century, it is thought
that this was hallowed ground well before
then. The temple takes the form of a pagoda,
an architectural form which originated in Nepal.
Pashupatinath is another name for Shiva, to
whom the temple is dedicated.

Ruins of the Buddhist Vihara

Paharpur, Naogaon, Bangladesh

In the far north-west of Bangladesh is the remote Somapura Mahavira Vihara at Paharpur. *Somapura mahavira* translates as 'great temple' and a *vihara* was originally a refuge for mendicant monks who might need shelter during bad weather. Paharpur means 'small hill', and this name came to be used because when the monastery was abandoned, it became overgrown and resembled a mound in the countryside. This is a humble shelter that became a great temple, which then dissolved back into the terrain to be eventually rediscovered. Now it sits poised between those positions – a monument to Mahayana Buddhism gently rising from the landscape in elegant geometry.

From the seventh century this place enjoyed at least 500 years of intellectual rigour and learning and is the largest known monastery south of the Himalayas. The temple was pyramidal, about 21 metres (69 feet) high, with a cruciform floor plan, around which 177 rooms acted as cells for the monks. The entire structure appears to have been richly decorated with ornamental terracotta tiles depicting deities, musicians, snake-charmers and fabulous beasts.

Mahayana or 'Greater Vehicle' Buddhism developed in response to the increasing number of lay Buddhists who could not devote their whole lives to the stringency of earlier practice. Instead, the notion of Bodhisattvas was introduced. These compassionate beings delay their own enlightenment to assist others on the road to salvation, and from that precept the pantheon grew to encompass a plurality of Buddhas, Bodhisattvas, deities and guardian spirits.

right The cells around the temple at Paharpur were once the backdrop to the orderly lives of Buddhist monks, and then later Hindus and Jains came here. Today, walking the geometric remains can be used in the same way as following a labyrinth or tracing a mandala. Though not laid out for that purpose, the angles and turns could be an aid to walking meditation.

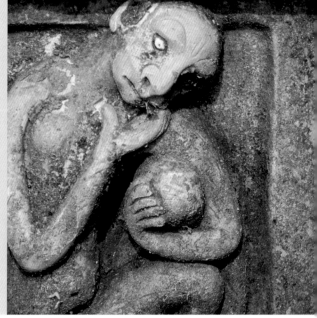

above It is easy to visualize the temple and its surrounds resembling a hill when abandoned and overgrown. At its height this was a bustling city-monastery and a hive of intellectual development, ritual and rhythm. Although it now seems almost clinically stripped and bare, its aesthetic simplicity exudes serenity, in contrast to the visual stimulation offered by busier sacred sites.

right Terracotta plaques were used to decorate the walls of the temple and although these are not highly sophisticated, the curvaceous lines are expressive and inventive. Traces of red and white pigments indicate that the images would have been quite colourful. Many movable objects are within the Paharpur museum for safekeeping, including columns, metal images, coins and inscriptions.

above The temple was built of bricks baked locally. Now grassed over, it was surrounded by cells, stupas, chapels, altars, wells and channels, all highly decorated. Considering the scale of this site, its construction must have been an enormous project. It is not clear what stood at the top of the temple – it may have contained an inner space or held a monument.

Ayutthaya
Ayutthaya Province, Thailand

Founded in 1350 by King Ramathibodi I, Ayutthaya (also known as 'Ayudhaya') became one of Asia's richest cities, replacing Sukhothai as the capital of Thailand, a status it enjoyed for over 400 years. The city's name derives from the Sanskrit word *ayodhya*, meaning 'undefeatable'. What is left is spread over a wide area, indicating the huge size that the city reached. Many of the statues and buildings are contained within an island, Koh Muang, formed at the confluence of three rivers – Chao Phraya, Pa Sak and Lopburi – which are linked by a circular canal. This made the city fertile and easily defendable. The location, close to the Chao Phraya estuary, lent itself to trading, and thus prosperity.

The King was considered a deity within the Buddhist tradition here; he was also patron of the arts and this manifests itself in the remaining monasteries, sculptures and *prang* (reliquary towers). Buddhist artists have long used a strict visual language to express spiritual potency to the full. The *prang* at Ayutthaya show a Khmer influence of gentle curves tapering to a point, while many of the Buddhas display the earlier Sukhothai style, in the pointed protrusion on top of the head, the *ushnisha*. The graceful physique and elongated earlobes imply wisdom and spiritual advancement. Eyes may be half-closed to signify meditation, their shape echoing lotus petals, while the eyebrows are arched and the line continues down to form the nose. The anatomy is minimally depicted; all is stylized to signify grace, serenity and compassion.

In direct opposition to those attributes, the city was destroyed during 1767 by the Burmese army. Much of the city's glorious art was looted, broken and burnt, but what remains resolutely smiles, transcending worldly worries with an undefeated spirit.

left Trees played an important role in the birth, life, enlightenment and death of Buddha and so they have come to represent enlightenment or *parinirvana*. The half-open eyes signify meditation and the hint of a smile on the lips indicates a recognition of truth. The lying position shows Buddha's final release from the cycle of rebirth at the age of 81.

above At the Wat Yai Chai Mongkol monastery, built in 1357, each Buddha has an individual face. They sit in the 'earth touching gesture', with one hand gently reaching down to represent the moment when the Buddha asked the earth to witness his faith and resolve in the face of extreme temptation. His concentration earned him the goal of enlightenment.

left The temple of Wat Phra Sri Sanphet was built in 1491 and at one time housed a 16-metre (52½-feet) high standing Buddha covered in gold. This was the main focus of worship in the *virana*, or worship room, until the invading Burmese army smashed it. However, these *prang* have been restored and their elegant lines add a transcendent beauty to the site.

right Here the fifteenth-century artists have given us the Buddhas in the 'gesture of meditation'. There is no attempt at anatomical detail; the Buddhas are depicted minimally, with linear simplicity to indicate serenity. Several of the *lakshanas* or '32 marks of a great man' are shown: level feet, a divinely straight frame and so on.

below The bas-relief carvings at Angkor Wat are the world's longest. The imagery is fluid, sophisticated and highly detailed and covers a wide-ranging content, with scenes from mythology and cosmography. The artists who executed this epic drew an astonishingly vibrant distillation from their materials, in keeping with the Hindu belief that everything contains the essence of the creator, who is present in all things.

Angkor Wat
Siem Reap, Cambodia

The Khmer Empire was ruled by Suryavarman II from 1113–1150 and it was he who built Angkor Wat, a temple dedicated to Vishnu, the Hindu preserver of the universe. The elaborate temple with its five towers sends ripples of splendour through its enclosing walls, out to the lawns and forest, through the majestic moat and on to the rest of the Angkor complex. Suryavarman's name for the temple is unknown but Angkor Wat translates as the 'city which is a temple'.

The layout of Angkor Wat is a microcosm of the Hindu concept of the universe. Symbolizing a mountain, three tiers support the temple: the first dedicated to the king, the second to the creator–god Brahma and the moon, and the third to Vishnu. Five towers are set in a quincunx, representing Mount Meru, the Hindu home of the gods. As detail and symbolism intensify on the approach to the centre, access becomes more

exclusive. While there is nothing unusual in this when measured against other sacred buildings, Angkor Wat reverses tradition in some respects. Elsewhere, Khmer temples are orientated towards the east; this one faces the setting sun. Furthermore, the elaborate narrative of the sumptuous bas-reliefs is told in anticlockwise order. Both of these aspects indicate that Suryavarman may have intended this as a funerary temple.

It was believed that the dimensions and design of a temple should honour the solar and lunar cycles, thus engaging in harmony with the cosmos. At Angkor Wat this is played out in linear measurement and the wall decorations tell tales of cosmic

above The climb to reach the 65-metre (213-feet) Central Tower is not for the faint-hearted, but today's visitors are privileged as originally access was exclusively for high-ranking priests and royalty. Its alignment is such that at vernal (spring) equinox the sun appears to rise out of the tower. The Tower of Echoes holds astonishing acoustics; visitors are invited to thump their chests and wait for the effect!

battles. Friezes have titles such as Heaven and Hell, The Churning of the Sea of Milk (Milky Way) and the Battle of the Gods. Culture was distilled in Suryavarman's mind and the ripples of his vision spread through priest-architects and artists to become the place that draws so much wonder from visitors across time and space.

Ha Long, Bay of the Descending Dragon Vietnam

Vietnam skirts the shores of the South China Sea and Ha Long Bay is 170 kilometres (105¾ miles) east of Hanoi, in the Gulf of Tonkin. Its name means 'Bay of the Descending Dragon'. Dragons feature largely in Vietnamese mythology, which tells that the Vietnamese people descended from a King-dragon who fathered 100 children through his coupling with a goddess. When the descendants of those children were defending their shores from foreign invasion, the Jade Emperor sent a Mother Dragon with a mighty army of Child Dragons to spit precious jewels, pearls and jade upon the enemy in a shower of shards. As these missiles hit the sea they formed a myriad of islands, so defending the land and thwarting the enemy. The people were happy and the dragons decided to stay in what was now peaceful and beautiful water. Today it is said that a dragon-like beast called the Tarasque still haunts the area.

As the scene of the country's origin myth, Ha Long Bay holds a sacred place in Vietnamese identity; it is stunningly beautiful and a uniquely diverse home to a broad spectrum of life forms, worthy of its place as a national treasure. Rich marine life teems in the sparklingly clear waters and the islands are a playground for antelopes, monkeys, iguanas and colourful bird life. Caves up to 30 metres (98½ feet) high shelter quieter life forms and shine with light bouncing off the crystal sea.

There are 1,600 substantially-sized islands with up to 3,000 smaller islets, and together they cover 1,500 square kilometres (579 square miles). This is an ancient landscape and human culture stretches far into prehistory here, so the roots of myth and tradition run deep, with many of the islands, caves and beaches having their own stories and mythologies that have been polished by the sands of time.

left Ha Long Bay is a place of myth and mystery and home to 60 coral species, 400 fish species and 140 seaweeds. These represent just a few of the gems found around these treasure islands. The bay boasts coral, lagoon and island ecosystems as well as a stunning aesthetic power, which fluctuates with the light and climate.

above Boats have been present in the bay since time immemorial and there was an important port for trade here by the twelfth century. Today the waters are busy with cruises and water sports as well as the fishing industry. The bay has been populated since prehistoric times with three distinct cultures emerging and leaving signs of their traditions for archaeologists to find.

above right The limestone islands rise from the surface of the water like fabulous beasts floating in a sea of jade. Such a sight will always inspire the imagination of storytellers and artists of all genres. Emperor le Thanh Tong came in 1468 and was inspired to extol the majesty of the area in a poem which he later had engraved on the Poem Mountain.

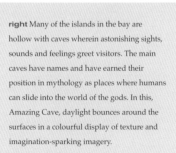

right Many of the islands in the bay are hollow with caves wherein astonishing sights, sounds and feelings greet visitors. The main caves have names and have earned their position in mythology as places where humans can slide into the world of the gods. In this, Amazing Cave, daylight bounces around the surfaces in a colourful display of texture and imagination-sparking imagery.

Borobudur Java

Java is the world's most densely populated island and so it is not surprising that it hosts a broad religious spectrum. The country's indigenous culture absorbed Shivism and Buddhism that came from India, though the majority of Javanese now follow Islam. In central Java, at a place whose full name, Bhumisan Brabadura, means 'The Ineffable Mountain of Accumulated Virtues', is the site commonly known as Borobudur. Built by the Sailendra dynasty, it dates from the eighth and ninth centuries and has its roots in Hinduism, but it is now a hugely popular Buddhist shrine.

The structure represents a three-dimensional mandala – a cosmographic model of a perfected world. It is constructed of six square platforms, beneath three concentric circular tiers, topped by a ring of 72 stupas around a single dome symbolizing oneness. In turn these levels represent the worlds of desire and animal need, form and then formlessness. The decoration on each platform is designed to express and assist those states. Therefore there is a simplification towards the top level, as the multiplicity of bas-relief images at the base gives way to unity at the top.

This site has no contained space; it is intended as a processional path climbing a sacred mountain, portraying the journey to inner enlightenment. The very structure guides pilgrims and worshippers up through the levels in a clockwise direction, allowing the right hand to keep contact with the shrine. This ancient practice is recorded in texts dating from the third millennium BC and it aims to awaken and connect with the divine by encircling it. By the time pilgrims reach the top they will have passed 2,672 bas-relief panels and 504 Buddhas, climbed countless stairs and accumulated ineffable virtues!

right A Buddha sits facing the sacred Mount Merapi, which erupted in 1006, shrouding Borobudur in ash. It stayed covered for 800 years. Annually, a priest climbs the 'Mountain of Fire' with a ritual offering as it embodies the home of ancient Javanese spirits and also Mount Meru – the mythical axis of creation for Hindus and Buddhists, and also the model for this shrine.

left Some of the bas-relief panels are biographical and narrative while others have a cautionary function, relating cause and effect. All flow from right to left so that they make sense to pilgrims walking clockwise up the temple. The 2,672 panels were carved in situ, after the temple had been erected. No mortar holds the stones in place, skillful cutting ensures stability.

top left Borobudur is the final destination of a processional ceremony to mark the Buddha's birth, death, enlightenment and escape from *samsara*, the cycle of reincarnation. Called Waisak, the event is held at the time of the Taurus full moon and is a national holiday. In this image we get a sense of the imposing presence of the building and the climb ahead.

above A Buddha sits within each of these 72 stupas and they encircle a single dome denoting oneness. This is the realm of Arupadhatu, the ultimate enlightenment where the soul escapes bodily form. The stupas are on three tiers and the dome on one higher. These illustrate four levels of meditation on the immaterial.

Ancient Building Complex

Wudang Mountains,
Hubei Province, China

The Wudang Mountains in China's Hubei Province are known for their concentration of Taoist monasteries and the sacred lives of those who lived in them. The Five Dragon Temple was the earliest sacred building to be constructed. It was completed in the seventh century, during the Tang Dynasty, although the mountain was almost certainly thought of as holy long before then, with worship taking place out of doors.

Taoism believes that nature itself is divine and that we should live in harmony with natural cycles and systems. Therefore the created world is to be revered. Mountains not only sustain a wealth of nature with their springs, caves, flora and fauna, they also support the sky and in so doing create the space in which life blossoms. The mountain complex spreads its dramatically beautiful landscape more than 30 square kilometres (11½ square miles). Mountain peaks give way to gorges and valleys; medicinal herbs

take their power from the soil; still, smooth pools lick around rough, dry rock and the sun casts shadow on the surface. These are the interdependent opposites that strive to maintain life's balance, epitomized in the yin-yang symbol that represents Taoism.

The Ancient Building Complex on the mountains was begun in 1412 during the Ming Dynasty, as a series of sacred and secular buildings for the advancement of knowledge and spirituality. It comprises palaces, Taoist temples and monasteries, pavilions and gateways. The devotional buildings were constructed and decorated with attention to discipline and symmetry, spaced to harness the powers of the mountain to such a degree that

above Standing at the top of a long flight of steps this, the Gate of Pilgrimage, is a welcome sight to lift the spirits and greet the weary traveller. Taoist architecture was designed with an eye to long life and eventual immortality; its makers hoped to work with a godly touch. Gates symbolically represent a goal – passing through admits the pilgrim to another realm.

echoes ring between the walls. From the earth, traditional Chinese herbalists picked over 300 medicinal herbs, while meditation, martial arts and the visual arts flourished, along with philosophy and all forms of Taoist disciplines. Many of those are still taught here today and tourists are welcome, but asked to tread gently.

above The Pavilion to Read Scriptures sits on Lingxu Cliff in Peach Wood Hill. Peach wood wards off evil spirits and so this place, being remote, verdant and blessed with spring water, hums with vitality and is ideal for withdrawal and contemplation. Chen-Chuan lived here for 20 years and developed the Dragon Sleeping Way, which enabled him to live to the age of 108.

above Dragon Head Perfume is a pair of ingeniously-sculpted mythical dragons lunging 3 metres (9¾ feet) out over a precipitous valley and facing the Golden Peak. In the distant past young men would show their courage and devotion by climbing onto the dragons' backs to burn incense. However, following a number of deaths the emperor forbade the activity.

above From the Golden Palace on top of Heavenly Pillar Peak, is a view of the many temples and halls in the building complex. The colour red has deep significance, representing the searing hot furnaces of the alchemists, whose endeavours to create gold from base metals symbolized the transcendence to which Taoism aspires.

Yungang Grottoes
Datong City, Shanxi Province, China

Chinese Buddhist artists of the fifth and sixth centuries made an astonishing artistic departure in the wonderful sculptures and carvings found in 252 caves in the south face of Mount Wuzhou. These are the Yungang Grottoes. They served as massive and powerful displays of Buddhism, both by the artists and the Wei Dynasty, who commissioned them. Buddha was not depicted in art until around the first century BC, his teachings prior to this were recorded symbolically rather than in narrative form. The images made at Yungang firmly established the visual language and identity of Buddhist art in East Asia. There are 51,000 statues and carvings of Buddha here, ranging from just 2 centimetres (1 inch) to 17 metres (55¾ feet) high!

Early texts record that the Toba Wei Emperor, Ming Yuan Di, used to pray at Mount Wuzhou before the cave project began, so clearly this was already a place of numinous power, to which the caves were a response. The tradition of cutting cave temples into cliffs came to China from India via Afghanistan and Central Asia. It was the monk Tan Yao who persuaded Emperor Wen Cheng Di to allow the project. Tan Yao began working on five of the caves around 460 AD but up to 40,000 people were involved for a period of over 60 years, many of whom were from the local community, but influences from India, Pakistan and Afghanistan played a key part, in the dress style, exotic flora, fauna and musical instruments, along with references to Greek architecture.

Over time war, weather and natural disaster have caused damage to the artworks, eroding paint and the stone itself. However, they are protected now and many have been saved from collapse by careful intervention from an even wider community than that which brought them into being.

right We can gain some insight into the effects of time and weather by comparing the inside of the caves with the façade, where erosion has eaten away both pigment and structure. This picture also gives an idea of the physical scale and chromatic range deployed by the artists and craftsmen.

above In Cave 3 the Buddha is attended by two figures. He sits with his right hand raised to shoulder height, palm facing out, in the fearlessness *mudra* (hand gesture) denoting spiritual power. It represents his ability to grant freedom from fear to others. Legend tells that Buddha quieted a raging elephant by making this simple mudra.

top right Mountains play an important role in the historical life of Buddha, and in Buddhist cosmology. To carve temples and statues into the rock itself honours those sacred traditions and magnifies the devotional site. Here the overall effect shows various aspects of Buddha's nature – conversing, teaching and preaching – each niche to be contemplated individually in order to understand the whole.

right In Cave 16 the standing Buddha's right hand is in the mudra of fearlessness, the left in the explanation gesture. This sculpture is badly weathered, the middle section being almost worn away, giving the figure a transcendental quality, akin to the incense smoke that rises outside the cave. Time has brought about a subtly constructive change.

Kii Mountains Honshu, Japan

The Kii Mountains on the Honshu island of Japan are thickly forested and have been revered as a hallowed landscape for over 1,200 years. Their still and flowing waters, and the spirits that dwell in the mountains and in the trees all generate a spiritual charge unlike any other. Three places in particular have been identified as being especially blessed with sacred power: Yoshino and Omine, Kumano Sanzan and Koyasan. These are strung along pilgrim routes between Nara and Kyoto and together they express the ancient and living religious traditions that have evolved from the syncretism of nature worship – Shintoism and Buddhism.

To the north of the mountain range, Yoshino and Omine have the oldest sacred tradition, having been home to the monk En no Gyoja and the followers of Shugendo, the ascetic mountain dwellers who studied and practised their faith within the forests from around the seventh century.

Kumano Sanzan is in the southern area of the range and has three shrines, each originally having a distinct style of nature worship. Over time these have become a Shinto-Buddhist fusion and the design of the shrines has influenced architectural forms way beyond the Kii Mountains.

Among the steep peaks and glades around Koyasan, 117 temples linked by a network of paths and pilgrim routes represent over a thousand years of worship. During 816 the Buddhist priest Kukai was instrumental in developing Shingon or 'True Word' Buddhism here, having visited and studied in China, bringing back texts and artworks. Shingon fully exploited aesthetics in the form of visual art, and ritual and sacred acts to emphasize and express beliefs. It is said that Kukai reached enlightenment and now lives in deep meditation in the Okuno-in Temple. The Kii Mountains are a sacred landscape marked and used by worshippers whose faith has been marked and formed by landscape.

right The feet of the verdant Kii Mountains interlock and accommodate one another in a manner akin to the fusion of faiths here; each has its own identity and interacts with its neighbours. The mountains occupy a peninsula that touches the Pacific Ocean and the spiritual landscape covers Shugendo, a Shinto-Buddhist syncretism, and Shingon Buddhism.

left The monk Kukai continues to be hugely
charismatic. Over 300,000 people are buried as
close as possible to his own grave here among
the ancient trees at Okuno-in, Koyasan. Stories
of Kukai's goodness and supernatural ability
abound. For example, it is said that he struck
the ground to bring a freshet of water to thirsty
villages, and that his spirit still lives here.

left below Trees are a valued part of the
cultural landscape throughout the sacred
Kii Mountains, and here they are carefully
integrated into the monastery complex at
Koyasan. Around 50 of the Koyasan temples
minister to visitors who are offered *shukubo*,
temple lodging. Overnight guests are invited
to share in early morning worship, as well as
shojin ryori, monastic vegetarian meals.

right The Nachi-no-Otaki Falls is Japan's
largest waterfall, with a drop of 133 metres
(436 ¼ feet). The Seiganto-ji Temple and
Kumano-Nachi Taisha – a Shinto shrine – are
here because of the sacred waters that are still
worshipped. There are sacred stones and trees
in the area too, all combining to give pilgrims
an intensely spiritual and sensory experience.

Mount Fuji
Shizuoka/Yamanashi, Honshu, Japan

With its iconic conical profile and snow-covered peak, the dormant volcano Mount Fuji is Japan's most famous natural landmark and its tallest mountain. Fuji-san is also known as the Mountain of Immortality, holding the key to eternity within its volcanic core.

Fuji was given its name by Japan's aboriginal people, the Ainu, and means 'fiery goddess'. The Ainu believe that everything in creation holds a spirit, and that spirits can determine natural events, therefore it is crucial to treat them with honour and reverence. Mount Fuji inspires faith among a variety of traditions and Shintoism, the Way of the Gods, also sees the divine in all of creation. Water springs from mountains and so mountains are bringers of life, nourishment and cleansing. It follows then, that deities must reside in these sacred places. To Japanese Buddhists, the perfect peak breaking free of the world symbolizes meditation, in which one rises above the everyday into another state of being, like the lotus flower reaching from the mud towards the sun. Mount Fuji is the home of the Cosmic Buddha, who is also known as Dainichi Nyorai, Vairochana and The Illuminator.

The syncretic faith Shugendo was developed by En no Gyoja. Shugendo followers lead an ascetic mountain life, eating herbs and following strict spiritual practice to attain magical powers. Shugendo lore claims that En no Gyoja was the first person to climb Mount Fuji, in around the seventh century.

At the end of the climbing season, flaming torches are lit in a fire ceremony held in honour of Konohana Sakuya Hime, a major Shinto goddess who is thought to give protection from fire and to ease childbirth. Many of Fuji's shrines are dedicated to the goddess and have been for centuries, so it is ironic that women were not allowed to climb the mountain until 1872. They were thought to cause bad weather by annoying the gods!

right Mount Fuji is a relatively young volcano in geological terms but on a human scale its sacred roots are ancient and varied. The mountain is a spiritual focus for many traditions and has been down the ages. *Sangu shinko* is the Japanese term for the belief that mountains are sacred, protecting animals while housing spirits and gods.

left The official climbing season is short, spanning July and August to avoid bad weather, so the routes can become crowded. However many choose to climb at night so as to reach the summit in time for sunrise, which can be transcendentally beautiful for hikers and pilgrims alike. Many draw great spiritual strength from stepping on this sacred ground.

right This *torii* has been placed to frame a view of Mount Fuji so two auspicious symbols are brought together into one picture, the sacred mountain apparently contained within the powerful vermilion gateway. Being at the crest of a hill, the position is a natural stopping point, inviting pilgrims to pause and take stock; once the vantage point is left, then the whole perspective alters.

left A *torii* is a symbolic gate marking the transition from the secular world to the sacred. Passing through, one is sanctified and it is usual to wash one's hands and mouth as a sign of cleanliness. At this Shinto shrine, pilgrims have left bells hung from ribbons of vermilion; the colour of life, marking the mountain of eternity.

australia & the pacific

The pages of this chapter reveal a range of unbuilt sacred places. Raw landscape is largely left to assert the spirit of place, in extremes of height and depth, fire and water. In fact, Rapa Nui and Raiatea are the only sites visited here that are marked by stone on stone. When Europeans first reached Australia, the indigenous people had a long-established religious culture, the Dreamtime, which had been present *ab origine*, or 'from the beginning'. As we shall see the Aboriginal spiritual activity relates closely to the natural landscape, from powdered earth to pooling water.

Tongariro National Park in the North Island of New Zealand holds a varied topography of snowy mountains, meadows, active volcanoes and craters. There are springs, lakes and volcanic desert. By definition then, this region is ever changing, due to all the dynamic climatic processes inherent in the landscape. It beautifully represents the extremes we meet in Australia and the Pacific.

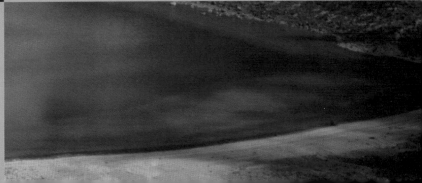

In calling themselves Maori, the people in
New Zealand nominated themselves as being distinct from the
wairua, or deities; the term *Maori* means 'ordinary' or 'natural'.
They reached the islands from eastern Polynesia and brought
with them the concept of *tapu*, which affirms a thing as being
sacred and therefore deserving of the utmost respect and
protection, perhaps even to the degree of being unspeakable
and unapproachable, for fear of desecration. *Tapu* can also imply
exclusion from some activities to particular groups. Maori priests,
called *Tohunga*, would use a declaration of *tapu* as a way of
protecting resources from overexploitation, and it is this notion
that many are now adopting, to varying degrees, as a means of
restoring ecological balance throughout the world.

For instance, the first destination here is the endangered Great
Barrier Reef, not only a sacred site but a sacred gift, with its
wonderful, watery beauty. By contrast, Lake Mungo is now
parched as a result of the prehistoric climate change, which
forced the population to move on. Weighing these two sites
allows us to revalue what we have and question how we can
sustain the natural world and pass it on to those who follow us.
It is startling to realize that since the middle of the last century
the average temperatures throughout Australia have risen
and rainfall patterns have changed too. Heartening to know,
however, that in 2006 the Climate Institute of Australia published
statements from 16 living faith traditions, beseeching a change
in behaviour to avert irreversible change in climate.

Another of our great gifts from God is artistic inspiration and the
ability to use art to express the ineffable, which was recognized
by the *ab origine* people when they made their first marks with
earthly pigment in their efforts to reveal the spirit world. Even
in these days of sophisticated digital imaging, many of today's
artists still feel the primordial thrill that comes from touching
pencil to paper and pigment to canvas; how much more magical
that must have been to our ancestors, free from the inuring
effects of today's rapidly changing images and media. And
what power must have been attributed to those who could coax
spiritual beings to manifest themselves through mark-making,
for as paint soaked into permeable stone, ethereal beings
emerged from those same pores. But there is even more to the
miraculous aspect of painted caves, cliff faces and canyons than
meets the eye. Throughout the world, sites with ancient paintings
and petroglyphs are also those rich in echo and other acoustic
phenomena; undecorated ones lack that apparently supernatural
quality. And it has been suggested that the sound waves caused
by chanting and droning would take visible form as patterns in
smoke. The visual and sound effects generated at these sites

anointed them as a point of contact with the spirit world, a portal, even, between realms. The experiences must have been perceived to be magical, metaphysical meetings. What other interpretation could there have been?

Believing that the creation spirits lived within the rock walls is established in Aboriginal lore and the paintings that depict them are formed accordingly. For instance, the Mimi spirits that are said to emerge from crevices and fissures within the rocks in Kadaku National Park are depicted as being thin and elongate to facilitate movement through those tiny openings. So we find visual and acoustic arts combining within the psyche to confirm and amplify spiritual presence and pass knowledge, through experience, to future generations.

The current guardians of Uluru link the past with the future too. They have put measures in place to continue the ancient Mala Law of the Anangu Aboriginal people, traditional owners of Uluru. Within the Bungle Bungle massif, elders protect the future by keeping parts of their knowledge within their own community. Some wisdom is considered too dangerous to circulate abroad, just as some locations would be defiled by the presence of outsiders; such learning is handed only to those deemed capable of both understanding it and safeguarding its future.

The idea of sending knowledge into the future by way of education and conservation relates to the concept of the sanctity of the natural world, where *tapu* automatically implies a responsibility of guardianship over the sacred. While it is easy to understand the desire to protect what seems vulnerable, when the idea is applied to a feature as forceful as a volcano, such as Ruapehu in Tongariro Park, then we can feel the power of commitment from a people who are proud to cherish its awesome presence rather than feeling cowed by it. Volcanic activity was also the force that formed Rapa Nui, where the dimensions of the universe are conceived as being split into horizontal and vertical planes; the light, sky world being linked to the dark underworld by the earth we tread upon.

Having begun this chapter at the wide sweep of the Great Barrier Reef crowning the huge country of Australia, we finish at the coral-encircled Bright Sky Island of Raiatea. Here stands Taputaputea, a doubly sacred place with the origin of the Polynesian gods at its core. To some, this is also regarded as the spot from which the first people emerged from the dark underground, to celebrate and care for our bright, sacred world.

opposite page Lake Mungo, Mungo National Park, New South Wales, Australia. **below left and right** Bungle Bungle, Purnululu National Park, Western Australia, Australia.

Great Barrier Reef
Coral Sea, Queensland, Australia

Millions upon millions of tiny organisms make up the enormous structure that is often called the world's largest organism. The Great Barrier Reef skirts 2,300 kilometres (1,429 miles) of the north-east coast of Australia and is home to countless species, rare and plentiful, within a unique ecosystem. Fisheries here have always supported communities of indigenous peoples down the ages and archaeological evidence, though not extensive, tells us that the area has spiritual and cultural significance for them. The richness of this heritage is magnified by the gorgeous grandeur that is so intense and supernormally beautiful as to defy description.

How is the sacred to be defined in something so large and varied? If the magnificence and diversity were not sufficient, then perhaps the thought of losing this to global warming and pollution may help us regard nature's bounty in a new light. Like all ecosystems, the Great Barrier Reef is a thread in the mesh that connects all life on earth, and in firing our senses, reminds us that sustainable living has to be a two-way process. Furthermore, we cannot claim to love creation if we destroy the resources that should be supporting the people, plants and animals that depend upon it. The Great Barrier Reef symbolizes all that is generous in nature and serves to remind us of the sacred duty of guardianship.

left This is home for many endangered and protected species, including marine turtles, whales, dolphins and dugongs. Today's indigenous peoples are involved in keeping the balance between traditional values and the use of resources, set against the increasing pressures that threaten the stability of the Great Barrier Reef, such as tourism, commercial fishing and climate change.

Lake Mungo Mungo National Park, New South Wales, Australia

In the Mungo National Park in New South Wales, is the desiccated Lake Mungo, long parched by prehistoric climate change. Along with signs of human occupation dating back perhaps 60,000 years, Mungo Man – Australia's oldest human remains – and Mungo Lady, subject of the earliest ritual cremation, were found buried on the south-east shore. These have been tentatively dated to those very early years.

The lakes of this region were once a bountiful source of nourishment and home to early people. The Mungo people enjoyed freshwater fish, mussels and land creatures, such as emus and probably the super roos, now extinct. Plant life was plentiful too, with the tubers and fruits of water lilies adding to the diet. The people camped by the lake and cooked their food over open fires. In time, the lake dried up and the Mungo people moved on.

Around the rim of the drying lake, clay and quartz sands were blown into crescent-shaped dunes, or lunettes, one of which is called the Walls of China. With yet more passing time, plant life colonized the shores. However, non-indigenous animals were introduced and stripped the vegetation, exposing the land to another onslaught of erosion. However, this time the shifting sands revealed the fireplaces, tools, artefacts and food remains that allowed archaeologists to piece together the Mungo people's story. It was at this time, in the mid-twentieth century, that Mungo Man and Mungo Lady were found. Two big mysteries still surround Mungo Man. He was buried turned slightly to one side, knees and elbows bent, hands clasped. Like European burials from the same period, his body was covered in red ochre, which is still used symbolically by today's Aborigines. However, here is the mystery – red ochre is not found in this landscape. Furthermore, his DNA has not been matched elsewhere.

right The Walls of China impart an unearthly atmosphere around Lake Mungo. The lake lends its name to Mungo National Park in south-west New South Wales. Along with other lakes in the area, it dried up in prehistoric times, having once supported Aboriginal communities. Clays are topped with quartz and soil that the lake left along its shores as water levels rose and fell.

above Evening shadows articulate the textures of the Walls of China around Lake Mungo. It is hard to imagine that this area once flowed with sufficient water to bring all types of plant and animal life to live here. As the waters dried up, strong prolonged winds created compact sand dunes that are now being gradually eroded, to reveal the signs of life left by early man.

above The area is a place of extreme temperatures that can easily exceed 40 degrees centigrade (104 degrees Fahrenheit) and drop below 0 degrees centigrade (32 degrees Fahrenheit) overnight. Visitors are therefore urged to take water and extra clothing. However, those lucky enough to use the camping facilities here have the joy of superb stargazing, free from light pollution, an activity surely familiar to the early Mungo people.

above Not a fossilized tree stump but a section of the eroding quartz sand dune. At one time in the area's recent past, sheep and rabbits overgrazed here. A series of droughts and storms wreaked further devastation. However, the park is being co-managed with the Aboriginal people and indigenous vegetation is fighting back, tempting animals and bird life to return too.

Uluru (Ayres Rock)

Kata Tjuta National Park,
Northern Territory, Australia

The Anangu Aboriginal people are the traditional owners of Uluru, the great mass of sandstone whose profile is widely recognized as a cultural and geographical landmark. The Anangu are thought to be one of the world's oldest societies and their belief system is intricately linked to this place.

There are many legends about Uluru, for example, that it came to be formed through the earth rising in grief following the deaths of tribal leaders in a battle. But one story resonates in particular, because of its link between traditional, contemporary and future matters. The Mala, or rufous hare-wallaby, used to live extensively in the area until about halfway through the twentieth century when it became extinct in the wild, in part due to urban pets and foxes. However, the Mala have been important creation beings to the Anangu and are deeply embedded in Anangu culture. For tens of thousands of years

the spirits of the ancestral hare-wallaby people, also called Mala, have been present in the very essence of Uluru and have guided and protected all living things.

In the early days, the Mala people travelled from afar to come here. On arrival, camps were set up in which the elders encircled the mothers with young children, to protect them. A ceremonial mast was erected high on Uluru and the rhythm of life harmoniously followed Mala law, Tjukurpa. However, people who wanted to disrupt the Mala system had created an evil canine beast called Kurpany. Aware of the plot, Luunpa, the kingfisher, called out a warning, only to be ignored. Two Mala

above The 348-metre (1,142-feet) high Uluru has stubbornly survived the erosion process that has erased the original mountain. Now there is a mountain's worth of power condensed into the sandstone and mythology that live on in this haunting place. It also has the astonishing ability to change colour according to time and season. Here, it glows gold against the azure sky.

men were killed and everyone fled. That was in the distant past. In the recent past, the Anangu and Uluru park rangers have collaborated to reintroduce the Mala wallaby, to ensure the long-term survival of the creature so significant to the continuing Anangu culture.

above These delicately painted plant forms look as indigenous as the lichens that grow naturally on the stone. Many of Uluru's caves hold rock art. Some of the images are ancient and some are recent, due to the act of working image over image to create a palimpsest of visual and spiritual information.

above Mutitjulu waterhole collects rainwater from the steep-sided basin into a pool that has been used by people and animals for thousands of years. Feeling the presence of so many at this source of life creates an almost tangible link with those who came before. This spot must have met countless needs for body, mind and spirit.

right From the air, Uluru resembles a flint arrowhead, yet seen from the ground it could clearly never take flight. However, in close-up, abstract sculptural forms are seen, which invite investigation into flights of the imagination and ancient culture. Visitors are asked to keep to ground level or to walk with a ranger to avoid disrupting the spiritually vital paths of the Mala.

Kakadu National Park
Northern Territory, Australia

Gagudju is the floodplain language once spoken in this area, from which Kakadu takes its name. Situated in the Northern Territory of Australia, the Kakadu National Park stretches roughly 200 kilometres (124 miles) north to south and 100 kilometres (62 miles) east to west. Its waterways, lowlands, hills, basins and caves are home to endemic flora and fauna and, for more than 40,000 years, to humankind too.

This sacred cultural landscape has evolved in response to the activities of the 'first people', the ancestors of today's Aboriginal population. The ancestors came in many forms and established the language, codes of conduct and ceremony that give this culture unique insights into the spiritual and physical landscapes. One aspect of the cultural heritage is rock art and the Mimi spirits were first to exploit this form of expression. When the Mimi portrayed themselves on the rock, this became a type of 'dreaming place'. Dreaming Places mark the Ancestors' activities and the sites at which they entered or left the earth. Some of these sites have arcane meaning and may only be viewed by a select few, because of the sacred and even dangerous values contained within. At Kakadu, the Jawoyn people are custodians of the sites and know which areas may be visited by all, and which should be left untouched by the public.

The art may depict hunting scenes to increase success and to commune with the animals' spirits. Religious rites were painted to reinforce their significance and creation stories may be shown to record and teach the myths and to influence the outcome of various events. Not only are the paintings considered sacred, but so too are the acts of making them and preparing the paint. One of the pigments, the iron-rich red ochre, known as haematite, resembles blood and so symbolizes life and reproduction, therefore holding the palette's greatest sacred charge.

right The sandstone rocks of Ubirr are Dreaming Places and hold a gallery of ancient rock art. The images were made and overpainted during a prolonged period, compressing time within the myths and stories. This stunning, raw landscape is a favoured place for watching the sunrise and to make contact with the spirit of creation.

left This otherworldly landscape is one of the most ancient sacred sites. Formed of molten lava, the Devil's Marbles are locally known as the Karlu Karlu and as the eggs of the Rainbow Serpent, one of the Creation Ancestors who made the Aboriginal people and the face of the world. Rainbow Serpent is associated with waters, fertility and relationships.

above The silky surface of Yellow Water Billabong at sunset belies the activity of the life it holds, for it is home to a broad spectrum of birds and fish, and their predators, the crocodiles. Kakadu is home to one-third of Australia's bird species, making it a treasured nature reserve as well as a mine of spiritual wealth.

right The Mimi spirits lived within rocky crevices and portrayed themselves on the walls outside their homes. Emerging on still nights to avoid wind damage, their thin bodies are shown as athletic hunters and energetic dancers. These are the ancestors who instructed the Aboriginal people in the arts, hunting and the codes of conduct.

Bungle Bungle Purnululu National Park, Western Australia, Australia

The Bungle Bungle is a massif within the Purnululu National Park. The 380-million-year-old sandstone has been carved and smoothed into a sculptural mass of mounds, their contours banded with orange and grey. The visual effect is an astonishingly hypnotic, whorling landscape standing 200–300 metres (656–984 feet) above a grassy and woody plain, giving way to pools and gorges.

This wilderness was once known only to the Aboriginal peoples who came for the lush hunting grounds during the wet season, buried their dead here and painted on the rock walls. For over 20,000 years the Aborigines were the only ones to enjoy this sacred landscape; until the 1980s it was unknown to the outside world. Dreaming Places are often at sites of extraordinary natural features, and as this is still a place of great significance, outsiders are asked to keep to the tracks and not to abuse their welcome.

Creation Stories are the wellspring of Aboriginal spirituality and very closely tied to the landscape, local waters, rock formations and other topographical phenomena. One area will have a different spiritual focal point to that of its neighbour, and only the local elders will understand why. In fact, cultural understanding is passed to individuals according to their particular needs, usually through rites of passage. Therefore outsiders will never have a full or clear understanding of the Aboriginal culture or where all of the hallowed sites are to be found. It also means that only the local tribes can have a complete understanding of their own definition of sacred.

Just as the elements were needed to expose the sculptures held within this landscape at the time of creation, the threads of Creation Stories woven around the Dreaming Places can only be interpreted by the traditional Aboriginal owners.

left Echidna Gorge has been described as one of Australia's most mysterious places, and as having one of the most particular atmospheres. For 20 million years the quartz sandstone has been gradually eroded by wind and weather to create a landscape that is awe-inspiring in its grandeur and epic in the way it displays the transient effects of light and shade upon solid stone.

above Often described as being like beehives, these conical forms, seen here from the air, stand up to 300 metres (984 feet) high. Biology, geology and erosion are the tools with which nature has created these sculptural forms of sandstone and algae, one of the highlights of the Bungle Bungle massif in Purnululu National Park, wherein ancient sacred sites are hidden.

above This is a dry riverbed on the plateau from which the Bungle Bungle rises. During the wet season this place has always offered an abundance of food to be hunted and gathered. It rings with the song of more than 130 bird species, from the colourful budgerigars to the brightly painted rainbow bee-eaters. As the light changes throughout the day, the landscape itself throbs with colour.

above For thousands of years, local Aborigines were the only ones to know about this area. Now they play a vital role in the shared management of what is recognized as being of great value to the rest of the world too. The Aboriginal culture locked inside, the unique aesthetic and the spiritual lift to be found in something so spectacular are terrific treasures.

above The conical forms of the Bungle Bungle massif are an extraordinary sight, especially when viewed from the air. The banding of the domes, due to differences in clay content and the porosity of the sandstone layers, is enhanced with the setting sun.

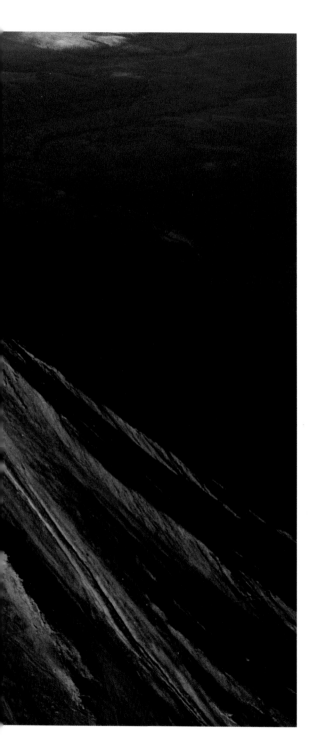

Tongariro Park North Island, Ruapehu District, New Zealand

Paramount Chief Te Heuheu Tukino gave a sacred gift of the central North Island peaks of New Zealand to the nation during 1887. The mountains have spiritual significance for the Maori people as they embody the community's sacred link with the landscape. The gift was made on condition that the area should be protected, particularly from exploitation by European immigrants. Mounts Tongariro, Ngauruhoe and Ruapehu hold particular spiritual magnitude. The chief's foresight led to Tongariro becoming New Zealand's first national park and so the *tapu* places are valued with due respect. To the Maori, and in Polynesian society, the term *tapu* is applied to something that is sacrosanct (see also page 224) and *tapu* things should not be approached, disturbed or, in some cases, talked about or looked at. (It is from this source that the term 'taboo' derives.) This concept has been used by priests and leaders to guard other resources from exploitation too, as within Maori culture it is a sacred duty to protect anything that is *tapu*.

Wahi tapu are sacred sites of burial, baptism, places where blood has been spilled, healing waters and pathways for the messengers. It goes without saying that outsiders may be unaware of the magnitude of the ground they are stepping on, looking at or photographing, so it is vital that visitors absorb as much information as is available before stepping off the well-marked tourist trails.

It is said that this region became volcanic when High Priest Ngatoroirangi prayed for fire during a snowstorm. He turned his thoughts to Hawaiki, the Maori's traditional homeland. The flames that came burst forth as volcanic eruptions, stopping at Ngatoroirangi's feet and forming the Pacific Rim of Fire, with this area on its southern tip. Thus Ngatoroirangi brought volcanic activity to the land and the Maori joyfully accepted this gift from the god, Ruamoko, who rules over the earth's fiery core.

left The conical peak of Mount Ngauruhoe shows steep sides and an imposing atmosphere. The Maori have ancestral ties with the mountains and they represent the earth's formation and man's emergence upon it. The powerful energies and spiritual power contained in creation is called *mana*, and it refers to that which cannot be described, but engenders a feeling of awe.

above The smoke from Mount Ruapehu is kissed by the morning light. To the Maori, the earth's fiery forces are a gift, rather than a thing to be feared. This is one of the world's most active volcanoes and the island's highest peak. Between eruptions it cradles an acidic crater lake.

left Lake Taupo is a *wahi tapu*, or sacred site, and was formed by a huge volcanic eruption about 26,000 years ago. The Maori call New Zealand 'Aotearoa', and they arrived here more than 1,000 years ago from their ancestral home Hawaiki, having ventured out in voyaging canoes. Hawaiki is the place to which many Polynesian cultures trace their roots.

right The Emerald Lakes on Mount Ruapehu are filled by melt waters, precipitation and hydrothermal fluids that feed in through the lake floor, bringing minerals that colour and acidify the water, while volcanic activity causes changes to the level and overall shape. This action is regarded by the Maori as being integral to its spiritual forces. Eating and drinking around the lakes are forbidden, to honour their sanctity.

Rapu Nui
Southern Pacific Ocean

Rapa Nui is sometimes called Easter Island, the name given to it in 1722 by the Dutch who landed on Easter Sunday. It is also known as Te Pito Te Henua, meaning 'navel of the world', which may refer to the islanders' idea of their geographical place or to the site's isolation from other features. Isolation is one of the most striking aspects of this small, intriguing place.

Hardship and the slave trade trouble Rapa Nui's history and culture. It is thought that the first settlers arrived in around 400–600 AD, and along with water and lush vegetation, they found materials from which to make the enormous *moai*, the iconic statues for which the island is famous. Rapu Nui society was Polynesian, with high status being accorded to the *ariki mau*, the great chief, who was descended from the gods. *Moai* were made by honoured craftsmen and placed on platforms within shrines

or *ahu*, where they represented a variety of deities. Being protective, most of the figures faced towards the population, rather than out to sea, their eyes being deeply carved and in some cases, inlaid with coral to activate the spiritual power, or mana, of the figure.

In addition to the *moai*, the people made sacred petroglyphs showing animals and anthropomorphic bird figures, representing Makemake, the Creator God. Makemake was animated in an annual ceremony to determine who would become Birdman for the coming year. Candidates for the position gathered at Orongo, on a knife-edge between a crater and a soaring cliff.

above There are at least 360 *moai* within *ahus*, or sacred shrines, on Rapu Nui. The *moai* represent the gods and, for the society that made them, brought a reassuring guardianship to this most isolated of islands. Ahu Tongariki is one of the largest of the shrines and holds some of the most massive figures.

While the priests' prayers for the success of the ceremony flew off to the gods, the candidates' chosen men swam to the tiny island of Moto Nui to seek the eggs of the Sooty Tern. The first candidate to receive an unbroken egg from his swimmer then reigned as Birdman for the year, having gained authority through the wings of sacred rite.

above There are thousands of rock carvings on the island, many of which represent the Tangata Manu, or Birdman, who played a crucial role in Rapa Nui society. Beyond these petroglyphs lies Motu Nui, the islet from which swimmers would have to retrieve an unbroken egg in the annual ritual to identify Tangata Manu for the coming year.

above The *moai* are dotted around the coast of Rapa Nui in a protective ring. Although many have fallen over the years, due to tidal waves and other phenomena, most have been re-erected. Carved from volcanic stone, some of the figures weigh up to 90 tonnes (99 tons). The huge task of sculpting, moving and positioning these great works indicates the value placed upon them; it is not known exactly how they were moved into position.

above The lip of Rano Rarku separates the fresh water it contains from the sea. This is the volcanic crater from which the *moai* stones were quarried. It lies in one corner of the triangular island, separated from the southern Pacific Ocean by its narrow rim that drops steeply into the water. It was from this ridge that the Birdman ritual was launched.

Taputapuatea
Raiatea, Society Islands, French Polynesia

'Bright Sky' is the meaning of the name Raiatea, the second largest of the Society Islands in French Polynesia. It is also known as the Sacred Island because this was the birthplace of the gods, and thus of the spiritual life of the people of Polynesia. One of the island's most hallowed sites is Mount Temehani, sacred to the god Oro and on its ground a unique flower blooms – the Tiare Apetahi. This draws people to sleep on the mountain's slopes, to hear the gentle noise the flower makes as it opens at dawn.

However, Taputapuatea is perhaps the most powerfully sacred spot on the island. This is a *marae*, a space set aside and marked

out with stone or wooden posts, for sacred and social purposes. It is said that the first people emerged from the ground at Taputapuatea, in the days when the island was called Havaiki. Taputapuatea was therefore considered so holy that when a *marae* was to be built elsewhere, a stone was taken from here and planted as a seed of sacredness, rather like passing light from one candle to another.

During the nineteenth century Christianity came to the area and the *marae* were abandoned. However, *marae* land is still held as *tapu* that is so deeply sacred that it cannot be built upon or used for other purposes.

above As at other *marae*, the ground that has been set aside as *tapu*, or sacred, is marked by a flat terrace surrounded by peripheral stones to create a sanctuary for religious rite and ceremony. Raiatea is surrounded by a coral reef spangled with pearl farms, while the deep Faaroa River cuts through emerald rain forest. The island has many sites of sacred and archaeological treasure, as well as an inspiring, uplifting beauty.

above left An ancient King stone stands marking the sanctuary at Taputapuatea. As the birthplace of the gods and the soil from which man first emerged, this site holds deep significance within Polynesian tradition. The people of the island were great seafarers and it was from this spot that religion radiated to the surrounding lands.

Index

Suggested Reading

A Comprehensive Guide to the Religions of the World (The Times World Religions), Martin
   Palmer, Times Books, 2002.

A Heart for the World: The Interfaith Alternative, Marcus Braybrooke, O Books, 2005.

Alone of All Her Sex: The Myth and the Cult of the Virgin Mary, Marina Warner, Vintage, 1983.

Bright Earth: The Invention of Colour, Philip Ball, Penguin Books, 2002.

Colour Travels Through the Paintbox, Victoria Finlay, Sceptre, 2003.

Faith in Conservation: New Approaches to Religions and the Environment, Martin Palmer with
   Victoria Finlay, The World Bank, 2003.

Gods in the Sky: Astronomy from the Ancients to the Renaissance, Allan Chapman, Channel 4 Books, 2002.

Islamic Art and Architecture, Robert Hillenbrand, Thames & Hudson, 1998.

Journey Through the Ice Age, Paul G Bahn, Facts on File, 1998.

Mapping Time: The Calendar and Its History, E G Richards, Oxford University Press, 1998.

The Maya (Los Maya Nacional de Anthropologia), Amalia Cardós de Mendéz, G V Editores, 1987.

Medieval Views of the Cosmos: Picturing the Universe in the Christian and Islamic Middle Ages,
   E Edson & E Savage-Smith, Oxbow Books, 2004.

Pilgrims and Pilgrimage in the Medieval West, ed. Diana Webb, I B Tauris, 2001.

Reading Buddhist Art, Meher McArthur, Thames & Hudson, 2004.

Sacred Britain: A Guide to the Sacred Sites and Pilgrim Routes of England, Scotland and Wales,
   Martin Palmer and Nigel Palmer, Piatkus Books, 1997.

Sacred Earth, Sacred Stones, Brian Leigh Molyneaux and Piers Vitebsky, Laurel Glen Publishing, 2000.

Sacred Imagery, Judith Millidge, J G Press, 1998.

The Atlas of Religion: Mapping Contemporary Challenges and Beliefs, Joanne O'Brien and
   Martin Palmer, Earthscan Publications Ltd, 2007.

The Many Faces of Faith: A Guide to World Religions and Traditions, Richard R Losch, Wm B Eerdmans
   Publishing Company, 2002.

The Oxford Dictionary of Religions, ed. John Bowker, Oxford University Press, 1997.

The Oxford Illustrated Prehistory of Europe, ed. Barry Cunliffe, Oxford University Press, 1988.

The Places In Between, Rory Stewart, Harvest Books, 2006.

The Poetic Edda, trans. Carolyne Larrington, Oxford University Press, 1996.

Sacred Earth: The Spiritual Nature of Our Material World, compiled by Sarah Clive,
   Baha'i Publishing Trust, 2001.

The Sacred East, gen. ed. C Scott Littleton, Duncan Baird Publishers, 2001.

The Sacred Place, Paul Deveraux, Cassell & Co, 2000.

The Temple, John M Lundquist, Thames & Hudson, 1993.

The World of Pilgrimage, George Target, AA Publishing, 1997.

World Religions: The Illustrated Guide, gen. ed. Michael D Coogan, Oxford University Press, 1998.

Author Acknowledgements

Warm thanks for help and encouragement to Harry Bird, Sue Booys, David Booys, Richard Booys, Brian Catling, Ann Hind, Stanley Hind, Adam Papaphilippopoulos, Ámbar Past, Tila Rodriguez-Past, José Angel Rodríguez González, Sarah Simblet, Holly and Tom Slingsby. The publishers would like to thank the following sources for their kind permission to reproduce the pictures in this book.

Picture Credits

Key: t=Top, b=Bottom, c=Centre, l=Left and r=Right

4Corners Images: /Borchi Massimo: 23r; /SIME/Pavan Aldo: 163; / SIME/Romiti Fabrizio: 191, 193; /SIME/Damm Fridmar: 182–3; / SIME/Kolley Horst: 184l; /SIME/Johanna Huber: 112–3, 114; / SIME/Ripani Massimo: 108–9, 250l, 251; /Amantini Stefano: 36t, 185
Alamy Images: /©Asia: 192; /©James Bartholomew: 78r; /©David Bowman: 194; /©Dinodia Images: 174; /©Ilya Genkin: 228–9, 230; /©Yoel Harel: 70r; /©Wolfgang Kaehler: 40r; /©Michael Klinec: 204bl; /©Yadid Levy: 176; /©David Lyons: 54; /©Peter McCabe: 64–65; /©Alain Machet: 125; /©Ron Niebrugge: 41; /©Photo Resource Hawaii: 253; /©Profimedia International s.r.o: 127; /©Rolf Richardson: 122; /©Sami Sarkis: 124–5; /©South West Images Scotland: 62; /©Frantisek Staud: 221; /©Steve Allen Travel Photography: 184r; /©Travel Ink: 146; /©Worldwide Picture Library: 61
Associated Media Group/©Peter Langer: 186–7, 188t, 189t, 188–9b
The Bridgeman Art Library: /Detail of the Portico de la Gloria with the Old Testament prophets (stone), Mateo, Master (fl.1168–88)/Cathedral of St. James, Santiago da Compostela, Spain, Joseph Martin: 94; /St. Thomas a Becket, from the Life of St. Thomas a Becket, Trinity Chapel Windows, c.1220 (stained glass), English School, (13th century)/ Canterbury Cathedral, Kent, UK, Paul Maeyaert: 58l; /View of the west facade, built 1738–50 (photo), Casas Novoa, Fernando de (c.1680– 1749)/Cathedral of St. James, Santiago da Compostela, Spain, Lauros/ Giraudon: 95
China Wudang Net: 206–7, 208l&r, 209
Corbis Images: /©Theo Allofs: 225r, 243; /©Paul Almasy: 131l; /©Archivo Iconografico, S.A: 86, 105; /©Jean-Philippe Arles/ Reuters: 79; /©Yann Arthus-Bertrand: 53l, 102–3, 104r; /©Craig Aurness: 82; /©Bettmann: 85; /©Christophe Boisvieux: 216t; /©Elio Ciol: 83, 100–101; /©Herve Collart/Sygma: 151; /©Dean Conger: 123t, 210–1; /©Richard A. Cooke: 32–33; /©Ashley Cooper: 57t; /©James Davis/Eye Ubiquitous: 69; /©Robert Estall: 90–91; /©Macduff Everton: 22t&b, 68, 10l; /©Michele Falzone: 155r, 156, 158, 204–5; /©Jose Fuste Raga/Zefa: 110l, 123b; /©Yves Gellie: 120–1; /©Farrell Grehan: 204tl; /©Carol Havens: 88; /©Jason Hawkes: 48–49; /©Tim Hawkins/Eye Ubiquitous: 46l; /©Chris Hellier: 93t; /©Gavin Hellier/JAI: 111l, 136–7; /©John Heseltine: 80, 92; /©Angelo Hornak: 58r, 59, 81; /©Jeremy Horner: 130; /©Dave G. Houser: 224l&r, 231l&r; /©Andrea Jemolo: 96; /©Wolfgang Kaehler: 15l; /©Catherine Karnow: 155l, 198–9, 201t; /©Everett Kennedy Brown/epa: 217; /©Christine Kokot/dpa: 200–1; /©Bob Krist: 56, 143l; /©Earl & Nazima Kowall: 111r, 140–1; /©Charles & Josette Lenars: 30r, 87, 110r, 126; /©Barry Lewis: 225l, 242l; /©Craig Lovell:

15r; /©Ludovic Maisant: 162r; /©David Muench: 10r, 11l&r, 34–35, 36b, 40l, 42; /©Tom Nebbia: 12–13; /©Richard T. Nowitz: 118–9; /©Tim Page: 180r; /©Sergio Pitmitz: 47r, 98–99; /©Chris Rainier: 152–3; /©Daniel Samuel Robbins: 159, 202–3; /©Robert Harding World Imagery: 137; /©Joel W. Rogers: 47l, 70l, 71; /©Fulvio Roiter: 8–9; /©Thelma Sanders/Eye Ubiquitous: 139; /©Skyscan: 46r, 52; /©Joseph Sohm/Visions of America: 38–39; /©Paul A. Souders: 235; /©Keren Su: 4–5, 154l, 168r, 197, 213t; /©Luca I. Tettoni: 154r, 190; /©Sandro Vannini: 135t, 138; /©Pierre Vauthey: 84; /©Patrick Ward: 57b; /©K.M. Westermann: 162l; /©Nik Wheeler: 147r; /©Peter M. Wilson: 19l; /©Adam Wollfitt: 93b; /©Michael S Yamashita: 220t; /©Jim Zuckerman: 168l
DK Images: 44–45, 106, 107, 119, 246b
FotoLibra: /Richard Ash: 238b, 247; /Bouki Boaz: 117; /Harry Fox: 157; /David Hogon: 201b; /Chris James: 77; /Marie-Laure Stone: 147l, 213b; /Guenter Lenz: 241; /Tom Lloyd: 24; /Sergey Lutskiy: 74l&r; / Gordon Nicol: 63; /Nigel Puttick: 89; /Julia Rich: 66–67; /Ulrich W Sahm: 116–7; /Pierre Sells: 196–7; /Dave Tait: 97l&r; /Graham Taylor: 226–7; /Edward Woods: 234l; /Rob Wyatt: 238–9
Getty Images: 76–77; /Kenneth Garrett/National Geographic: 20–21; /The Image Bank: 16, 170–1; /Katsumasa Iwasawa/Sebun Photo: 214–5; /Stone: 17, 222–3; /Taxi: 27b, 31
Jon Arnold Images Ltd: 78l, 160–1
Kenneth Garrett Photography: 128–9
Lonely Planet images: /John Banagan: 242r; /Ross Barnett: 26; /John Borthwick: 252–3; /Tom Boyden: 239; /Mark Daffey: 115, 144–5; / Krzysztof Dydynski: 212; /John Elk III: 19r; /Greg Elms: 181; /David Else: 135b; /Peter Hendrie: 248–9; /Richard I'Anson: 177, 236–7; / Richard Nebesky: 18; /Oliver Strewe: 244–5; /Jim Wark: 36–37; / Woods Wheatcroft: 14; /Ariadne Van Zandbergen: 132–3, 134
Magnum Photos Ltd: /Ferdinando Scianna: 250tr
National Geographic: /James P. Blair: 250br; /Jason Edwards: 232–3, 234r; /Martin Gray: 104l; /Karen Kasmauski: 218–9, 220b; /Winfield Parks: 131r; /Michael S Yamashita: 6, 178–9
OnAsia.com: /Aroon Thaewchatturat: 167; /Agustinus Wibowo: 165
Photolibrary.com: 51; /James Emmerson: 50; /Imagestate Ltd: 246t; / JTB Photo: 28–29; /Japack Photo Library: 43; /Steve Vidler: 30l
Picture Desk/The Art Archive: San Francesco Assisi/Dagli Orti: 101t&b
RIA Novosti Photo Library: 72–73, 75
Rex Features: /Wildtrack Media: 240
Robert Estall Photo Agency: /David Coulson: 1, 148, 148–9, 150
Robert Harding Picture Library: /Tony Gervis: 169; /Gavin Hellier: 143r, 173r, 194–5; /Sybil Sassooon: 142; /Jane Sweeney: 164, 173l; /Alvis Upitis: 216b; /John Wilson: Front & Back Endpapers, 166, 172, 175
SuperStock: /©Ben Mangor: 2–3, 24–25
Three Blind Men/Dominic Sansoni: 180l
Topfoto.co.uk/2004 Charles Walker: 53r
V.K.Guy Ltd: 60
Werner Forman Archive: 27t

Every effort has been made to acknowledge correctly and contact the source and/or copyright holder of each picture and Carlton Books Limited apologizes for any unintentional errors or omissions which will be corrected in future editions of this book.